Teaching for Critical Thinking

Geraldine Van Gyn,
Carole Ford,
and Associates

London, Canada

**STLHE
SAPES**

Society for Teaching and Learning in Higher Education
La société pour l'avancement de la pédagogie dans
l'enseignement supérieur

STLHE Green Guides

© Society for Teaching and Learning in Higher Education, 2006
Third printing, April 2007

Distributed on behalf of STLHE by:
> The Book Store at Western,
> University Community Centre,
> The University of Western Ontario,
> London, Ontario N6A 3K7

Library and Archives Canada Cataloguing in Publication
Van Gyn, Geraldine 1949-
> Teaching for Critical Thinking/Geraldine Van Gyn, Carole Ford and Associates

(Green Guide; No. 6)
Includes bibliographical references and index.
ISSN 1718-2115   ISBN 0-9738227-1-6

1. Critical Thinking – Study and Teaching (Higher). I. Ford, Carole, 1942 - II. Society for Teaching and Learning in Higher Education. III. Title. IV. Series: Green Guide (Society for Teaching and Learning in Higher Education); No. 6.

LB2395.35.V35 2006   370.15'2   C2005-907859-6

Cite as:
Van Gyn, Geraldine and Ford, Carole (2006). Teaching for Critical Thinking. London, ON: Society for Teaching and Learning in Higher Education

Foreword

It is with great pleasure that I present *Teaching for Critical Thinking*, the sixth monograph in the Green Guide Series of the Society for Teaching and Learning in Higher Education (STLHE). This important Guide, written for college and university teachers, is first and foremost the work of Geraldine Van Gyn and Carole Ford of the University of Victoria. Geri and Carole would readily recognize, however, the vital support of several Associates and many members of the UVic faculty in the development and writing of this pedagogical Guide. In fact, a salient feature of this exploration of introducing critical thinking to students in higher education is undoubtedly the fact that it is born of an extensive, cross-campus discussion of many aspects of this issue at the University of Victoria. *Teaching for Critical Thinking* is, then, the fruit of a stimulating process of educational development as well as the result of many years of research, reflection and experience on the part of authors recognized for their leadership in this field.

True to the spirit of the Green Guide Series, *Teaching for Critical Thinking* captures the essence of literature on the topic without unduly dwelling on the findings of the latest research. The aim of the Guide is to provide practical advice on teaching for critical thinking across the curriculum. A significant number of tables in the Guide illustrate specifically how the various features of teaching for critical thinking can be introduced in a variety of disciplines. These tables provide useful references for professors in higher education who are at the various stages of implementing teaching for critical thinking strategies in the college classroom.

The Society for Teaching and Learning in Higher Education has sold many thousands of Green Guides since the appearance, in 1998, of Allan J. Gedalof's *Teaching Large Classes*. We expect that Green Guide No 6 will be as well-received as was *Teaching with Cases*, by David Dunne and Kim Brooks, published in 2004.

The STLHE Green Guide Series is patterned after the successful publications of our sister organization, the Higher Education Research and Development Society of Australasia (HERDSA). Dr. Christopher Knapper of Queen's University, the person who introduced the idea to Canada, is recognized as the Founding Series Editor. Carol O'Neil of Dalhousie University and Eileen Herteis of Mount Allison University became Associate Series Editors in 2004, and Roger Moore was welcomed to the team in a similar capacity in 2005.

Over the last year there has been a marked increase in interest expressed in the Green Guide Series. Not only has this interest been reflected in sales, but it has also led to a number of excellent proposals for future Guides. We now have no fewer than eight projects and proposals at various stages of development! To handle this increase in activity we have recently created an Editorial Board of enthusiastic and qualified volunteers from Canadian institutions and beyond.

Green Guide No 6 also marks a new chapter in the production and distribution of the STLHE Series. I would like to thank the Centre for Learning and Teaching, Graphics, and the University Bookstore of Dalhousie University for seven years of dedication to Green Guide preparation, printing, distribution, sales, and accounting. Without the volunteer efforts of many at Dalhousie, this Series would not have enjoyed such great success. The torch has been passed to the capable hands of Debra Dawson and Steve Alb at the University of Western Ontario, our new centre for Green Guide production and sales. Many thanks to the UWO team for stepping in to give the hardworking folks at Dalhousie relief after several very productive years.

Coming to grips with what it means, in practice, to stimulate and to implement Scholarship of Teaching and Learning theory and practice may be regarded as the new millennium's most significant movement designed to improve the quality of higher education. The Green Guide Series forms a tangible part of STLHE's firm commitment, expressed in programmes and policies, to furthering SoTL objectives. The Editors of the STLHE Green Guide Series are proud to contribute, on a voluntary basis, their time and resources to this worthwhile enterprise.

W. Alan Wright
Series Editor
For the Editorial Team

About the Authors

Geraldine Van Gyn

Geraldine Van Gyn is currently the director of the University of Victoria Learning and Teaching Centre and a professor in the Faculty of Education. Her research activities include studies of the educational benefits of cooperative education, development of expertise in high-level coaches, and the nature of effective practice. The core of her eclectic research program is the study of effective learning environments. In her 26 years at UVic, teaching for critical thinking has been the foundation for all her courses.

Carole Ford

Carole Ford has an MA in Curriculum and Instruction (University of British Columbia, 1988), and a PhD that focused on teaching for critical thinking (University of Victoria, 1998). She has taught elementary school in BC, worked with the Critical Thinking Consortium producing publications for teachers, and currently is a faculty member in the Faculty of Education at the University of Victoria. Carole integrates critical thinking into all of her classes.

Contents

Acknowledgements

This Guide is the culmination of the intensive questioning and careful thinking by a number of people. As members and friends of the UVic Learning and Teaching Centre, we began our collaboration on teaching for critical thinking in 2002 with a panel presentation at the LTC by Conrad Brunk (Centre for the Study of Religion in Society), Smaro Kamboureli (English), and Cornelia Bohne (Chemistry) on disciplinary perspectives. We thank these three academics for their willingness to make their thinking on critical thinking transparent and to debate with each other on the apparent differences. Based on the 'gems' that came out of that panel presentation, we felt that there were many other UVic faculty who could also help us to progress in our understanding of critical thinking. We interviewed 15 faculty who are well known for their teaching excellence and commitment to critical thinking. The outcome of these interviews was invaluable in helping us to identify some of the difficulties faculty face when teaching for critical thinking as well as some examples of best practices. Those faculty who were involved in the interviews were: Gweneth Doane (Nursing), Jan Zwicky (Philosophy), Smaro Kamboureli (English), Christopher Thomas (History in Art), Tim Hopper (Physical Education), Andrew Weaver (Earth and Ocean Science), Helen Raptis (Curriculum and Instruction), Judith Mitchell (English), Cornelia Bohne (Chemistry), Taiaiake Alfred (Indigenous Governance), John Green (French), Peter Keller (Geography), John Kilcoyne (Law), Margaret-Anne Storey (Computer Science), and Anne Irwin (Anthropology). We extend our sincere thanks to each of these academics for their contribution to the project.

From their many examples, we selected three to use as examples in the Guide. These particular examples were chosen as they each reflect a different level of complexity and draw upon quite distinct aspects of critical thinking. To Christopher Thomas, Anne Irwin and Gweneth Doane, we extend our thanks for their permission to include their examples in the Guide. As well, we used a specific example from the Calibrated Peer Review website and thank the administrators of the site for their permission to reprint from this source.

We include four people as our associates in the writing of this Guide. Carole Thibault conducted and transcribed all of the interviews and was instrumental in helping us think through how to reflect in the Guide the many perspectives that emerged. The contribution to this process of Yolanda Olivotto, programme co-ordinator in the LTC, was also invaluable. As a skilled critical thinker, she asked many challenging questions that required us to bring more clarity to our work. Richard King (Pacific and Asian Studies) and Gweneth Doane (Nursing) were our 'critical friends' throughout the process of preparing the Guide and were always willing to give us the necessary reinforcement or critical challenge to keep us moving towards completion of the manuscript.

Lynn McAlpine of McGill University introduced us to a curriculum design process that is documented in *Rethinking Teaching in Higher Education* (A. Saroyan & C. Amundsen, Eds.) published in 2004 by Stylus. The process of preparing to teach for critical thinking used in this Guide is based on the fine work of Lynn and the other contributors to the 2004 publication. We hope we have translated their course design model in the way it was intended.

Finally, we extend our sincere appreciation to the editors of this Green Guide for their thoughtful feedback and patience and to the anonymous reviewers whose suggestions contributed most positively to the final outcome. Seeking clarity about critical thinking takes time and requires multiple perspectives!

Introduction:
Teaching for Critical Thinking

Educating for critical thinking (CT) is vital to ensuring that university graduates are knowledgeable individuals who will engage in life-long learning as reflective, responsible, and effective members of society, professions, and families. A well developed capacity for CT is both an ideal and an essential outcome of higher education, an outcome that will not be achieved without specific and sustained attention to ways in which we teach.

In addition to the benefits of proficiency in CT for life after college or university, CT is a powerful way of enabling students to "work the content" (Case, 1997a, p. 143) both in their area of study and in new contexts. As such, CT is central to effective learning (Bransford, Brown, & Cocking, 2000) as well as a vital outcome of education.

Definitions of CT range from those that assign it to the particular use of specialized knowledge in a disciplinary area of study to those that characterize it as a general approach to the framing and solving of problems. The long history of well-documented philosophical debates on these and other issues associated with the understanding of CT dates from the time of Socrates. However, many instructors still struggle with ways to ensure that CT is embedded in student learning.

Teaching for CT requires constant reflection. The definition, dimensions, and criteria that we present in this monograph are working terms that are not fixed. We expect to modify these as we gain further experience with students and instructors in teaching for CT. To begin, then, our working definition of CT is as follows:

> A quality of thinking that is characterized by self-regulated deliberations
> on a challenge situation or task that involve exploring and generating
> alternatives, and making evaluative judgements. These judgements are
> based on criteria, which provide justifications for the conclusion, and are
> applied to meaning, relational, empirical, or value claims.

The extended and extensive nature of CT will emerge in the course of the discussions and applications of teaching for CT developed in this monograph.

We will follow applications of teaching for CT – definition, dimensions, criteria and assessment – in considerable detail in instructional activities from four different existing courses. Some instructors may find such detail unnecessary but the detailed applications provide clear and specific indicators of the intellectual decisions required for integrating teaching for CT. Engaging in these explicit decisions brings together instruction and assessment in interdependent ways that enable students to develop facility and proficiency in CT.

Those who teach in higher education have already developed expertise in CT and are acutely attuned to the intellectual traditions that characterize their particular disciplines or fields of study. Our aim in writing *Teaching for CT* has been to provide instructors with a conceptual framework and a set of conceptual tools (Saroyan & Amundsen, 2004) for designing and integrating teaching for CT in their courses. Central to our exposition of such planning are the applications of how this framework and the tools have actually been used. In concentrating on teaching for CT, instructors will find it necessary to reflect on and be explicit about their understandings of CT in implementing instructional change. This process directly involves the dialectical character of CT, which simultaneously deepens both understanding of CT and its application in instructional activities.

The title of this monograph tells readers about the emphasis and focus we bring to this subject. The title is *Teaching for CT* and not the teaching of CT. We believe and demonstrate that engaging students in CT can be integrated into any course, provided that the instructor takes the time and gives appropriate thought to designing and developing the course to include specific CT instructional activities.

It is also important for readers to understand what *Teaching for CT* is not. First, it is not intended to enable instructors to design a course with the principal focus and subject matter of teaching CT and nothing else. Second, the focus is not principally or generally on pedagogical issues as such, though pedagogical considerations can be found throughout. The approach describes the design and the implementation of 'a pedagogy for CT.' Through an explicit description of the nature of CT, through designing instructional strategies and appropriate forms of assessment, and through detailed applications, we present a methodological framework that enables instructors to transfer expertise and understanding into their teaching practice. The following summary of the content and organization gives the reader an overview of this monograph and the topics of its seven sections:

Section 1
Critical Thinking Instructional Design Process: A Framework
This section provides a rationale for an explicit CT instructional design process and for the learner-centred orientation that is crucial in teaching for CT.

Section 2
Critical Thinking Instructional Activities
This section describes four specific instructional activities in different courses that promote student engagement in CT.

Section 3
Definition and Dimensions of Critical Thinking
To introduce the first phase in the CT instructional design process, we discuss ways of thinking about CT and some key dimensions.

Section 4

Critical Thinking Criteria and Related Learning Outcomes

Having established a definition and the related dimensions of CT, the next step is to describe criteria for the dimensions. Criteria are the descriptors critical to success in implementing and assessing CT.

Section 5

Instructional Strategies to Facilitate Critical Thinking

In this section, we describe general instructional strategies and considerations in using these strategies.

Section 6

Assessing and Evaluating Critical Thinking

To facilitate the assessment design phase of the framework for CT instructional design, we include a discussion and examples of standards and rubrics for assessing and evaluating student proficiency in CT.

Section 7

Course Climate and Conditions for Supporting Critical Thinking

Courses that support CT encourage questions, dialogue, and the uncovering of multiple perspectives in ways that respect differences. We include an overview of factors that promote student learning through CT.

The detail we have provided on our conception of critical thinking required a considerable amount of work. We recommend that instructors start the process of incorporating CT into their courses by identifying one or two discrete instructional activities as the starting point for the engagement of students in CT. Instructors can then determine learning expectations for a small part of the course and gradually plan instruction so students can meet the learning expectations throughout. This gradual approach allows instructors to gain personal understanding of the components of engaging students in CT and how to bring instructional and assessment approaches without introducing a great amount of uncertainty for instructors and students. Our advice is to start small, but to start. We hope that *Teaching for CT* will both show instructors ways to incorporate CT in their instructional activities and encourage them to begin the process.

Critical Thinking Instructional Design Process: A Framework

A willingness to risk experimentation in one's teaching is an important aspect of modeling change and promoting critical openness in learners.

Brookfield, 1987, p. 81

Challenges to Teaching for Critical Thinking

Enabling students to develop a capacity for CT is challenging, both for instructors and for students. By using the approach and methods outlined in this Guide, instructors will be better able to introduce, plan, and integrate CT into their regular courses. Although significant time and considerable effort are involved for instructors, the systematic use of CT throughout courses will prove rewarding for instructors and for their students.

Being Explicit

It is important to define CT clearly in order to teach it effectively. It is also critical to set criteria and standards to assess CT. This need for clarity and precision may be, in itself, one of the most demanding aspects of teaching for CT, but it is also one of its significant benefits. For students to value the process of engaging in CT and for instructors to know that students are progressing, it is essential that assessment link directly to learning. To design ways of fruitfully assessing student development in CT, instructors must have a clear vision of: (1) how CT is constituted and applied within their disciplines; (2) the desired learning outcomes; and (3) the assessment criteria needed for judging the quality of these outcomes. Instructors must be able to clearly communicate these processes, outcomes, and assessment criteria to students.

Teaching for CT involves flexibility. Making the characteristics and expected outcomes of CT clear and explicit does not imply that instructors should be rigid or that they create a prescription for student work that leaves students achieving pre-determined and limited ends. Rather, teaching for CT requires openness and flexibility within a series of suggested frameworks. This approach requires instructors to offer explicit guidance to students, enabling the learners to progress as critical thinkers while encouraging them to make informed judgements on their own. Instructors for CT recognize and respect that, because of the complexity of most problems, effective critical thinkers draw upon multiple ways of addressing a particular problem, leading to different yet justifiable outcomes.

Those who teach in higher education have developed expertise in CT in their fields by practice, experiences, and models in undergraduate and graduate programmes. Rarely are professors (except perhaps for those who studied philosophy) asked to make explicit their practices and understanding of CT. Given the complexity of CT, individual instructors may find it difficult to 'tease apart' the concept and may, in fact, be reluctant to do so. Instructors cannot expect students to learn and to value CT if a definition, criteria, and standards for assessment are not made clear to them.

To fail to provide criteria and standards of assessment is like sending students on a journey with neither a form of transportation nor a destination while assuring them that the instructor will let them know when they arrive. An argument can be made that provision of guidelines or frameworks limits creativity and exploration of alternative ways of thinking, with the consequence of limiting learning. Although this argument has some merit, it is our experience that in the early phases of learning for CT, substantial guidance is crucial to progress. As students grow in their practice and understanding of CT, this need for guidance diminishes. A constant balance must be struck between too much structure and guidance and too little and insufficient support.

Providing Opportunities

CT will not develop in an intellectual vacuum, for acquiring facility and confidence in CT requires extensive and comprehensive practice. Unless those who teach provide recurrent, challenging, and meaningful opportunities for students to engage in CT and to critically reflect on their activity, students may develop an abstract or nominal understanding of CT but still be unable to engage in effective CT practice.

Many modern educational theorists argue that one of the most significant impediments to practicing CT is the long tradition of lecturing as the dominant form of teaching in undergraduate education. Student passivity, which is roundly criticized, seems to be reinforced by the lecture format. Yet increased class size, particularly in the first two years of university or college, has led to the widespread perception among faculty that lecture formats and reduced numbers of assignments and assessments are necessary coping strategies.

As a result of such demands, faculty spend the bulk of class time teaching students *what to think* rather than enabling them to learn *how to think*. It has been suggested that faculty often feel non-traditional methods that facilitate CT take too much time and produce anxiety for both instructors and students. Many professors assume that teaching for CT requires non-traditional methodologies. Tsui (2002) has confirmed that student engagement in writing and discussion, two traditional educational activities, are crucial to improvement in CT. As the extent and kinds of writing and discussion used influence the degree to which students can develop CT, the challenge is to use them more intentionally, explicitly, and frequently. To do so may require a decrease in the breadth of content included in a course. Too often we sacrifice the opportunity for students to reflect and to discuss the course issues in order to 'cover' all the content. Finding the balance between breadth and depth of learning is an important step in providing students the opportunity to engage in CT.

Planning for Critical Thinking

Because the intent of the Green Guides is to provide practical support to university and college faculty, we have identified, from research and our own experience, the main challenges facing the instructor in *teaching for CT*. The first challenge is the very notion of **CT** held by the instructor. Hence it important that a **definition** of **CT** be established and its **dimensions** provided. The second challenge is identifying the necessary **criteria for CT** and the measurable results that indicate students are successfully developing **CT**. From these criteria, we can formulate **CT learning outcomes**. These must be explicit so that students have a goal and a way of assessing their own progress. The third challenge is the choice of **instructional strategies** that provide opportunities for students to engage in CT. This means designing educational activities, both in and out of class, to give students ample practice for engaging in CT. The last challenge is **assessment of CT**. This is resolved to a significant extent by the development of criteria. However, it requires the instructor to review the types of assessment used in the course. The assessment instrument must give the instructor valid and reliable evidence of students' capability to engage in **CT** and allow discrimination among the levels of capability of demonstrating **CT**. To enable clear discrimination among the levels of student success, the instructor must also set standards for the established criteria. It is important to remember the planning involved in teaching for CT can be considered within the same framework as overall planning of instruction.

Figure 1 (see page 18) provides a graphic representation of the framework for designing the activities, necessary elements, and stages for instructors in the planning and developing of courses in which they make teaching for **CT** integral to, and a major objective and outcome of, their courses

In the next section we will present assignments or activities from four university courses to serve as examples of how the process of designing instructional activities can make teaching for CT integral to learning in different fields.

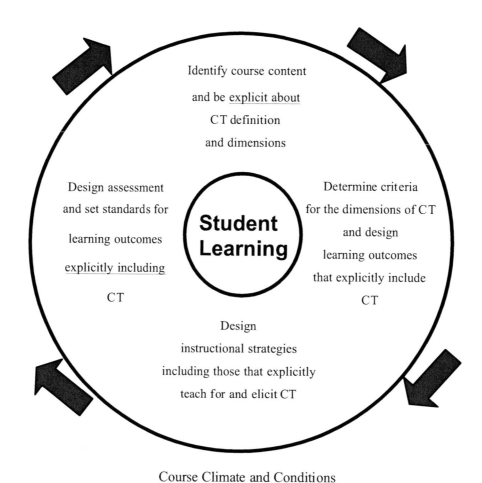

Identify course content
and be explicit about
CT definition
and dimensions

Design assessment
and set standards for
learning outcomes
explicitly including
CT

Student Learning

Determine criteria
for the dimensions of CT
and design
learning outcomes
that explicitly include
CT

Design
instructional strategies
including those that explicitly
teach for and elicit CT

Course Climate and Conditions

Figure 1. A framework for the process of instructional planning that includes teaching for CT as an explicit process and outcome.

Critical Thinking Instructional Activities

We have intentionally chosen four examples of instructional activities that represent different disciplinary approaches and subject matters. These examples, not difficult to implement, allow us to suggest how courses might be modified for use in a variety of fields of study. While none of these instructional activities appear to elicit the full scope and range of critical thinking, they do demonstrate how instructors can undertake the process of embedding teaching for CT into their students' learning activities.

1. Calibrated Peer Review in First Year Chemistry

Calibrated Peer Review (CPR) is an electronic instructional tool developed from the science model of writing and reviewing research proposals (Reference CPR Website: http://cpr.molsci.ucla.edu). The purpose of CPR is to allow students the opportunity to write short essays on specific topics and to ascertain, with appropriate guidance and criteria, the quality and calibre of what each student, along with three peers, has written on the same topic. Each assignment includes learning goals, source materials, student instructions, guiding questions, a writing prompt, and calibrations for essays of high, mid, and low quality. Each CPR assignment has four stages:

1. Research and writing. With guidance, students use resources to learn about, and to construct a short essay on, a particular aspect of the course content.

2. Learning. Students learn about criteria as well as process for successful writing from content and process perspectives. They practice the application of criteria and process by analysing essays of varying quality that have previously been evaluated and scored.

3. Peer review. Students review three peer essays using the criteria and process learned in stage 2, providing feedback and developing justification for that feedback.

4. Self-assessment. Students review their original short essays and subject them to the same criteria and process for assessment and scoring that they applied to their peers' essays.

These four stages are described in more detail in Table 1 below.

Table 1
General Description of Calibrated Peer Review Assignment

Text Entry: Stage 1	Calibration and Review: Stages 2, 3 and 4	Results
Students are presented with a variety of assignment – specific resources such as websites, textbooks, pictures, and movies to use in writing their essays. Students are also encouraged to explore additional resources. Students complete their essays and then move to the second stage.	Students are presented three essays on the same topic that have already been reviewed and scored by the professor. These essays are calibration essays, each representing a different caliber of performance from high to low, based on established criteria. Students answer a series of questions that will determine how well they understand the criteria and performance standards for the specific assignment. Students learn to recognize the strengths and limitations in the sample essays. If they are not successful in evaluating each of the sample essays, they are to reread, rethink, and reevaluate until they demonstrate that they fully understand what is expected in the assignment. If they are successful, their next step is to evaluate three essays written by their peers following the same procedure. Students then provide authors of the three peer sample essays with their evaluation ratings and justifications for the scores. Finally, students self-assess using the same performance standards. By this time students are familiar with the content and the expectations for the assignment, as they have completed a review and evaluation of six essays on the same topic.	Students receive immediate feedback when they check out the Results section to compare their responses with the professor's responses. Students are able to see how well they evaluated the essays of their peers. They see peer ratings for their own essay. An overall score out of 100 points is generated for each student, including points for the quality of their own essay, the quality of calibrations, the quality of peer reviews, and the quality of their self-assessment.

Table 2 provides the specific details of a CPR assignment for first year Chemistry.

Table 2
CPR Assignment: Electrochemical Restoration of Sunken Treasure

Assignment Goals	Source Reference Materials	Student Instructions	Guiding Questions	Writing Prompt
To explore a web site that describes both the wreck of the ship "Atocha" and some of the objects found in the shipwreck. To read a passage that describes the chemistry that caused a layer of silver sulfide to form on the silver objects, and to do further reading in the textbook on redox reactions, oxidation states, electrochemical principles, and electron transfer. To formulate a plan to electro-chemically remove the layer of silver sulfide from the silver object. To write an essay that describes how to use electrochemistry to "clean" the silver treasures from the "Atocha". To evaluate essays for fit with relevant criteria.	Website: URL:http://www.atocha1622.com/Atocha%20Story.htm Follow the Treasures of the Atocha link to read more about the shipwreck and see pictures of some of the treasure that was recovered. Check out HTML Tutor to help format your essay. General Chemistry Textbook: To answer all of the guiding questions, individual research will be necessary. The chemistry textbook should contain all the information about electrochemical cells, oxidation states, and what occurs when silver reacts with hydrogen sulfide. This will be the best resource for deciding how to restore the coins to their original, shiny state.	Read the following passage carefully. Afterwards, you will be asked to do some further research on your own, and then to write a short essay. A sample of the text follows…: Many ships have been destroyed in the past several hundred years by hurricanes, reefs, and other means. Sometimes they sank with holds filled with millions of dollars in gold, silver, and gemstones. The objects were restored using an electrolytic cell. It is your task to determine how this was done. You will need to use your textbooks or other resources on electrochemistry to figure out what the components of an electrolytic cell are, and how you would set up these components. You do not need to provide details (such as the composition of the solution used, or the exact type of electrodes), but you will need to describe the general set-up. Think in particular about where the coin (or other silver object) should be placed in the cell. You do not need to be concerned with any chemical process or equation other than the Ag_2S being changed back to $Ag(s)$.	The intention of the guiding questions is to stimulate critical thinking and to help you organize your thoughts about the topic. In studying the resources and writing your text, consider the issues raised by the following questions: What happens to the oxidation state of silver when it reacts with H_2S (aq)? What is this change in oxidation state called? How do electrolytic cells work? What happens at the anode? At the cathode? Where do the electrons flow from and to in the cell? In an electrolytic cell, does the reaction happen spontaneously, or does energy have to be put into the system? How could an electrolytic cell be used to recover $Ag(s)$ from $Ag_2S(s)$? Where would the silver object have to be placed in the cell? A random by-product of the electrochemical recovery process was the production of $H_2(g)$ at the surface of the coin. Suggest how this could aid in the cleaning or restoration process.	Write a paragraph of the required length suggesting how the $Ag_2S(s)$ layer on a silver coin could be converted back to $Ag(s)$ in an electrolytic cell. As you write, make sure to address the issues raised in the guiding questions. Also, remember that you are writing an integrated paragraph, not just answering a list of questions.

2. Role-Playing in First Year Anthropology

Role-playing requires that students assume the role of another person and enact a particular situation in class. Typically students are given a scenario or challenge from which they must gather information as part of making a decision, resolving a conflict, or coming to some conclusion. Table 3 below describes the elements and activities involved in the Nomad Game. (Contact Dr. Anne Irwin, University of Victoria, British Columbia, Canada. anneirwin@shaw.ca)

Table 3
Role-Play in Anthropology: The Nomad Game

Assignment Goals	Reference Materials	Student Instructions	Guiding Statements	Debriefing
To be an active learner in class. To respond to a conflict by adopting the roles for two different tribal groups in order to determine patterns of behavior and to solve the conflict by developing strategies for the negotiation process. To become comfortable with chaos.	Students are assigned to even or odd numbered groups, each group to represent either the Agriculturalists or the Pastoralists. Each group is given information that includes some background, the problem, social factors, cultural factors, and the instructions. Background information fully describes the nature of the tribe in regard to the location where members of the tribe live, the nature of the soil, environment, climate, and the occupation of the tribal peoples. The problem addresses some history of conflict between the Agriculturalists and the Pastoralists. Social factors include the protocol for communication and the relationships between men and women. Cultural factors refer to how each tribe feels about strangers, their attitudes toward nomads, and some of their customs.	Break into random groups with 5 to 8 students per group. Appoint an observer/recorder to watch the game and take notes. Even numbered groups are called the Agriculturalists (cultivate fields of barley, wheat and millet). Odd numbered groups are called the Pastoralists (herd flocks of sheep and goats). Each group is to carefully read a set of instructions specific to its tribe and plan a strategy to resolve the conflicting problem. Members of each group must consider all the resource information that is available while they deliberate on how to preserve the safety of the crops and water supply (Agriculturalists) or how to renew the right to use the grazing land on the way to winter pasturage (Pastoralists). Even and odd groups review the problem, determine their strategies and spend 30 minutes in negotiation.	Before the exercise, students are encouraged to have fun and think creatively. As part of their instructions, they are also told to make up cultural and social factors as needed. They are also to be prepared to debrief and discuss their experiences with the class. During the role play, the professor walks among the tribes and stimulates thinking by probing...*tell me what's going on here. What do you think might be the reason for this? Have you thought about this?*	The debriefing exercise helps students and the instructor to evaluate the role-playing exercise. Discussion is facilitated by questions from the instructor: How did the tribes reach agreement? What was observed about the different cultural norms? What problems did you encounter? How did it feel acting as a member of the tribe? What kinds of assumptions were made about certain norms/beliefs?

3. Reflective Reading Reports in Third Year History of Art

Although reading assignments are a regular part of university courses, many professors wonder whether their students understand the content and grasp the subtleties and nuances well enough to make connections, find meaning, or identify missing pieces. Reflective reading reports employ a series of questions to help focus student thinking and interest in the readings. These questions vary and are usually broad enough to appeal to various levels of learner interest and capability. Typically, there is neither a single correct answer nor one answer obviously more appropriate than others. Because students have to explain the thinking process by which they developed answers to the questions, they are encouraged, even prodded, to engage in higher-order thinking. Table 4 describes the elements and activities involved in the reflective reading report in an upper level History of Art course. (Contact Dr. Chris Thomas, Professor, Fine Arts, University of Victoria, British Columbia, Canada. christhomas@uvic.ca)

Table 4
Reflective Reading Report: The New Art History--A Critical Introduction

Assignment Goals	Reference Materials	Student Instructions	Guiding Questions	Evaluation
To provoke student interest in course readings. To develop familiarity with contemporary art-historical theory. To engage students critically with difficult material. To use student feedback/responses for guided discussions. To improve student writing skills.	Book: *The New Art History: A Critical Introduction* by Jonathan Harris	Read the assigned chapters from Jonathan Harris' book. Every week, develop a thoughtful question that the chapter raises for you. Submit your thoughtful question. Once you have completed the book, answer the guiding questions. *"Ideas don't exist until they are written."* – (Chris Thomas)	What three ideas or issues are worth remembering from this book? Explain how you decided on the three issues. What two issues or ideas do you need to follow up on or find out more about? Explain how you came to this conclusion. What is one burning or troublesome question? Explain how you will find the answer.	This is a formative writing process and therefore not graded. However, students are asked to consider the following criteria in the process: 1. A thoughtful question has clarity and structure. 2. Clarity is achieved when the question is not ambiguous or open to misinterpretation. 3. A thoughtful question would elicit an opportunity for analysis, comparison and contrast, cause and effect or reflection.

4. Audiotaped Interaction in Fourth Year Nursing

The audiotaped interaction is an unscripted and spontaneous recording made with a classmate focusing on a particular life experience or situation. The purpose of the audiotaped interaction is to provide an opportunity for students to experience a real life scenario with a "client" in order to analyze, reflect on, and question their current relational practice in nursing. The role of the students is to connect with their classmates, to facilitate the conversation, and to be relationally responsive to their experiences. A series of guiding questions for a reflective written piece invite students to observe and reflect on their approaches and responses, illuminate their taken-for-granted beliefs and assumptions that inform their approaches and responses, and consider critically the effectiveness of their interpretations, responses and actions. "Through CT, past actions and events can be reinterpreted from a new vantage point and new possibilities explored" (Gweneth Doane, personal interview, March, 2003). (Contact Dr. Gweneth Doane, Human and Social Development, University of Victoria, British Columbia, Canada. gdoane@uvic.ca)

Table 5 documents the application of the audiotaped interaction strategy in a fourth year Nursing course.

Table 5
Audiotaped Interaction Assignment in Nursing

Assignment Goals	Reference Materials	Student Instructions	Guiding Questions	Evaluation
To experience an authentic "client" interaction. To practice and reinforce "relational skills for the nursing profession". To help clients find meaning in their experiences, whether positive or negative. To engage students critically as they reflect on the way they engage and relate to others.	Analysis Sheet: This sheet is a template for students to record their verbatim dialogue. The sheet includes four areas: 1. What the Client Said 2. My Response 3. My-in-the-Moment Analysis (internal thoughts, feelings, my intent in responding, beliefs underlying my intent, values in use) 4. My Reflective Analysis (internal thoughts, feelings as I listen to interaction; alternate values that would enhance helping; alternate intent; alternate helping response) A concrete example is provided for each area of the analysis sheet so that students are clear about what is expected.	**Part I Baseline Tape 40%:** Make a 10-15 minute spontaneous, unscripted audio-taped recording with a classmate who is willing to talk about an experience she/he is having that presents some form of challenge. You are to take the role of nurse in this interaction. Use the Analysis Sheet provided to transcribe verbatim a 5 to 7 minute consecutive segment of interaction. In order to provide appropriate feedback, please use the template provided. Listening to the language that was spoken and the discourse that occurred, describe the relational connection and give examples to illustrate your description. **Part II Final Tape 60%:** Make a 15-minute spontaneous, unscripted audiotaped recording with a classmate who is willing to talk about an experience she/he is having that presents some form of challenge. In this part, you do not need to transcribe the tape. Re-listen to your baseline tape and then to the final tape, paying attention to the relational capacities you portray in each of the interactions. Following the transcription and analysis, reflect on the interaction overall and respond in writing to the guiding questions provided. Summarize how your relational capacity has been enhanced over the past few months.	**Part I Baseline Tape:** What was the nature of the "power and control dynamic" within this dynamic? What was your response to this client? What values-in-use were evident in the way you interacted with your client? How were your values-in-use congruent or incongruent with your espoused values? **Part II Final Tape:** What stands out for you as you listen to the two interactions? What changes did you notice in regard to your relational practice? What and how did your language change? Was your focus different in the two conversations? What did you do differently from the first to the second tape? Consider the relational capacities you learned about in the course. What did you notice about your capacity for initiation, authenticity, and responsiveness? What is the rhythm between dialogue and silence? How are you empathetically attuned to the person and the experience? In what ways do you foster an understanding of the meaning of the client's experience? How was that intent reflected in your approach and way of being? In what ways do you think you could continue to enhance your relational capacity and your ability to help?	Criteria for evaluation of the audiotaped interaction include: initiative, authenticity and responsiveness; mutuality and synchrony; honoring complexity and ambiguity; intentionality; re-imagining. Criteria for the evaluation of the analysis include: depth of analysis; critical thinking and synthesis of ideas; consistency of thoughts throughout the paper; completeness; as well as organization and clarity. Letter grades are assigned based on two clear descriptors of two levels of performance: (B- to B+) and (A- to A+).

These four model courses in which we have outlined some ways of teaching for CT lead directly into the next section in which we offer a definition and some of the dimensions of CT.

Definition and Dimensions of Critical Thinking

I would be content if we began, all of us, by recognizing that . . . discovering how to make something comprehensible to (our students) is only a continuation of making something comprehensible to ourselves in the first place.

Jerome Bruner, quoted in Ramsden, 1992, p. 150

Because CT is so deeply imbedded in what we do as scholars and what we hope for in student learning, we routinely assume that our students understand what CT is and how to explain and express that understanding in written, visual, and oral presentations. More often than not, this is an erroneous assumption.

Students need to develop an understanding of CT together with suitable, accurate and informed vocabulary of the dimensions of CT so that they can discuss with their peers and instructors their understanding and practice of CT. In addition, they need to be able to interpret feedback appropriately so they can modify and improve their understanding and practice of CT. This section presents some specific perspectives on the definitions, dimensions, and criteria involved in teaching for CT.

Definitions

The word 'critical' appears to have two roots in Greek (Paul, Elder, & Bartel, 1997): "kriticos" -- discriminating judgement, and "kriterion" -- criterion. Thus, the etymology of CT can be understood as pointing to the central feature of making discriminating judgements with reference to criteria, a process that Lipman (1991) calls "cognitive accountability" (p. 118). Cognitive accountability implies self-regulation so that those who engage in thinking critically suspend judgement in the face of insufficient evidence. Clearly, they may also change their position, perhaps many times, if the evidence so warrants. Judgements, as the outcome of CT, are purposefully determined and are integral to forming values and engaging in direct actions. The criteria upon which such judgements are based are guides in deliberations on the critical situation or task under scrutiny, and provide justification or reason for decisions (Ford, 1998). In contrast, the failure to engage in CT involves the absence of a deliberate quality and attention to criteria for judgements.

For many students the word "critical" has a pejorative meaning, one that implies finding fault with the materials they read or with the presentation they hear (Halpern, 1998). A comprehensive definition of CT must emphasize making an informed judgement that includes an explicit rationale as the basis for the judgement a student makes when reflecting on a reading, presentation, or other artefact.

Conceptually, CT has been associated with higher order thinking, decision making, problem framing and solving, reflective judgement, reflective practice, and a myriad of other intellectual activities. Definitions abound in the literature [see, for example, Brookfield, 1987; Ennis, 1996; Garrison, 2004; Kurfiss, 1988; Langsdorf, 1988; Lipman, 1991; Scriven & Paul, 2001].

For the most part, theorists attempt to express the dimensions of a particular kind of thought that will enable students to avoid conventional misunderstandings, misleading notions, and literalism (Endres, 1996) and will encourage them to challenge conventional suppositions and positions. We agree with Brookfield (1987) that CT should not be "a wholly rational or mechanical activity" (p. 12). In students' initial introduction to CT in a structured and intentional way, however, CT will most likely appear to them as overly rational, devoid of feeling, and even mechanical. As students learn about CT and become more conversant with it through practice, the elements and dynamics of the process will become embedded in their thinking and CT will take on a more fluid and flexible character for them. CT involves dialectical thinking, or thinking stimulated by and directed at understanding and struggling to make judgements in the face of contradictions or because of dissatisfaction with current thinking. CT also includes development and consideration of alternative solutions and ideas. CT is essentially a dialectical process. Much of the challenge in teaching for CT arises because students experience, at least initially, uneasiness and even anxiety with the give and take involved in arriving at sustainable judgements.

Our current working definition of CT, as stated earlier, stresses a quality of thinking characterized by self-regulated deliberations on a challenge situation or task, involving the exploration and generation of alternatives, and making evaluative judgements. These judgements are based on criteria, which provide justifications for the conclusion, and are applied to meaning, relational, empirical, or value claims.

This definition implies that in our teaching for CT we expect students to take a position about proposed meaning, about relationships, or the interactions among propositions, about explanatory or empirical claims, or about value or worth. In teaching for CT, then, it is essential to provide opportunities for students to confront issues, situations, or problems that invite multiple responses rather than a single and/or specific individual response. The ambiguity or uncertainty, even though it frequently unsettles students, encourages more complex thinking about the situation and the evidence/reasons, enabling students to recognize that there is typically neither one 'right answer' nor the perfect solution.

The use of the word 'judgement' may suggest that students are encouraged to sort out all the imprecision in the evidence and determine 'the truth.' In fact, guided by this definition, we encourage students to be mindful of the ways in which they accept or reject information, how they use the information, and the manner in which they come to a position. They also need to understand that, with further inquiry, their position may change. Central to this working definition is the focus on the quality of their thinking. Through CT, students may become more aware that the status of knowledge is not constant.

In Table 6 below, we indicate how each of the examples presented in section 2 aligns with our working definition of CT.

Table 6
Congruence of Examples with Working Definition of CT

CT Definition	Chemistry	Anthropology	History in Art	Nursing
The self-regulated deliberations on a challenge or problematic situation	Evaluate plans/essays for congruence with calibrated essays about how to electro-chemically remove the layer of silver sulfide from silver objects.	Reflect on strategies to respond to the tribal conflict over conflictual uses of land.	Critically reflect after reading an art text in order to identify important or interesting issues/ideas and questions for further inquiry.	Reflect back on the quality of their nursing responses as they critically consider an audiotaped discussion between themselves and a client.
that involve consideration of generated or selected alternatives	Analyze congruence among calibrated samples, peers' essays, and own essay.	Brainstorm alternative solutions to avoid an impasse in the negotiations.	Analyze relative importance or interest of issues or ideas in text.	Re-examine assumptions, beliefs and thinking that shaped their interpretations and responses during the interaction and consider alternative ways of responding in action.
directed towards evaluative judgements.	Judge clarity, comprehensiveness and accuracy of their peers' essays, and their own essays, about plans that will effectively remove silver sulfide from silver objects.	Judge what negotiation strategy will be most effective in solving the tribal conflict.	Judge what issues, ideas, and questions are personally most important or interesting.	Appraise the adequacy of their interpretations and responses within the context of promoting client health and healing.
Judgements are based on criteria, which provide justifications for the conclusion.	Criteria for judgement are embedded in questions and standards for levels of attainment are illustrated in 3 calibrated samples; students judgements and justifications regarding congruence among these criteria, relevant standards, and essays should be plausible and comprehensive.	A satisfactory outcome of the negotiation process is based on coming to consensus about a solution that has plausible potential to work as it is safe, fair, and doable; decision needs to be congruent with knowledge of tribal norms, customs, culture, and habits of each tribal group.	Issues, ideas, and questions should address ideas for which the outcome would matter to someone; ideally, students' justification for choice will be plausible regarding why idea matters to someone.	Judgment about the value of their interactions with the client is plausible in congruence with criteria that have been derived from theoretical and practice-based research toward effective practice.

Dimensions

Attending to the dimensions of CT is helpful for students in understanding the hidden complexities of CT not immediately evident in a working definition. In our model for CT, we include three dimensions: intellectual habits, intellectual deliberations, and a reflexive disposition. These are represented in Figure 2 below. Each of these three dimensions contributes to the dynamics of student engagement in CT and, ideally, we should be able to find evidence of all three dimensions in student responses.

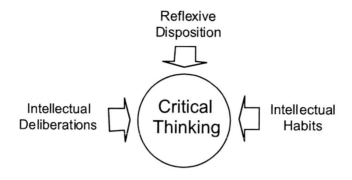

Figure 2. Graphic illustration of dimensions of CT.

1. Intellectual Habits

These intellectual habits are qualities of thinking that consistently characterize careful responses to challenge situations or tasks that involve engagement in CT. These intellectual habits include: intellectual curiosity, respect for truth and reason, fair and open mindedness, tolerance for ambiguity and complexity, intellectual courage to take a position, intellectual work ethic, and willingness to engage in collaborative inquiry.

We use the term *habit* to indicate that students need to develop and display these attributes in their academic work with consistency. The term *habit*, however, is not intended to suggest mindless or routine activity. These habits are attributes of CT that instructors can model, discuss, and reinforce with students at any level of learning.

2. Intellectual Deliberations

These intellectual deliberations include the following: identifying the challenge situation or task for inquiry; gathering, understanding, and interpreting background information and other evidence; applying relevant thinking strategies; making judgements based on relevant criteria; and constructing justification for judgements.

Intellectual deliberation influences the numerous formal ways of thinking, learning, and knowing. Each or several among the multiple ways of conducting inquiry has a distinctive home in one or more disciplines or areas of study, though rarely in all. Garrison (2004) suggests that disciplines appear to have distinct ways of constructing and organizing knowledge and characteristic emphases on particular ways of knowing and thinking.

Intellectual deliberations as a dimension of CT are influenced by the particular mode of inquiry of the discipline or field in which CT is practiced. With reference to the roots of the word "critical," as discussed above, and the understanding that particular modes of inquiry have specific intellectual criteria, we suggest that learning to think in a critical manner within a particular area of study requires acquisition of the types of deliberations for inquiry that characterize the intellectual tradition and practice of that field. Within a field of knowledge, the forms of intellectual deliberations and the modes of inquiry are integral parts of a whole.

Table 7 below is an illustration of how intellectual deliberations can be applied in practice across three familiar modes of inquiry. This representation is not intended to be comprehensive but rather to offer several examples of the varied ways that the aspects of CT are evident in these modes of inquiry.

Table 7
Examples of intellectual deliberations in three modes of inquiry

Main Intellectual Deliberations	Fundamental Questions of Inquiry[1]	Empirical Inquiry	Interpretative Inquiry	Critical Inquiry
Identifying the challenge or situation for inquiry AND applying thinking strategies relevant to the type of inquiry.	1. What is my purpose in pursuing this issue?	To determine causation and facilitate prediction	To deepen and elaborate on meaning and understanding	To engage in action to enable emancipation and social justice
	2. What is the central question and why is it significant to this type of inquiry?	Significant questions are derived from theory…	Significant questions arise out of contradictory positions and evidence	Significant questions arise from evidence of oppression, inequity, and power imbalance
Gathering and interpreting background information AND applying thinking strategies relevant to the type of inquiry.	3. Have I considered all of the evidence and reasons that are likely to impact on my question?	Have I included the breadth of empirical research that has been conducted that is related to my question?	Have I reviewed all of the conceptual research or perspectives relevant to my question and considered them in sufficient depth?	Have I received input from all of those who might be affected by the outcome of the inquiry and have I considered alternative perspectives?
	4. What assumptions am I making?	I need to ensure that my interpretations of the research do not have any bias.	I need to pay attention to any assumptions that I do hold and make it clear how they shaped my understanding.	I need to challenge assumptions in order to interrupt or perturb any constraining ideology or discourse.
	5. What evidence or reasons will influence my perspective?	I will consider evidence that is valid and reliable.	I will consider evidence that has credibility, is trustworthy, and reflects rigor in the methodology.	I will consider evidence from relevant voices or perspectives that have been left out and are required for social action.
Generating or selecting alternatives	6. How will I interpret the evidence?	Through statistical analysis	Through content/conceptual/ linguistic analysis	Through critical analysis
AND making judgements among alternatives based on criteria relevant to the kind of judgement	7. What alternatives are generated by the evidence or reasons?	What evidence counts against or for the conclusion? What other possible conclusions might be made?	What other interpretations are possible? Which interpretations are stronger, more inclusive? Which interpretations represent key ideas necessary and sufficient to the conclusion? Which make key ideas salient? Which conclusion has the most integrity, utility? Which conclusion is morally preferable?	What other voices have been omitted? What is the impact of the perspectives that have been included? How do these perspectives inform or limit my understanding?
AND justifying conclusions based on sufficiency of evidence and reason as well as congruence among evidence, reason and conclusions.	8. Which alternatives are more defensible or sustainable?	What sources have more validity and reliability? What evidence is stronger? What evidence, if any, counts against conclusion?	What interpretations are stronger i.e., more plausible, inclusive, congruent, relevant, sufficient?	Which views are more morally justifiable, i.e., acceptable, inclusive, safe, fair; feasible?
	9. What are my main conclusions and how will I justify them?	Deductive reasoning	Inductive reasoning that raises a moral question	Inductive reasoning and moral reasoning

[1]These aspects were derived from the work of Richard Paul (Foundation for Critical Thinking [http://www.criticalthinking.org])

3. Reflexive Disposition

Research and other ways of knowing can themselves become ideologies. McPeck (1990) states that, "Rational beliefs as well as rational methods are fallible, after all, and the critical thinker is acutely aware of how and why this is so." (p. 16). Therefore a third dimension, a reflexive disposition, is needed for students to fully engage in CT. This dimension includes the self-regulated capability to plan ahead for CT, monitor its quality throughout, and reflect on the strengths and limitations of intellectual deliberations and on the use of intellectual habits in making a judgement. A reflexive disposition involves stepping back or "decentring" (Habermas, 1990) from personal requirements, disciplinary or social norms, and personal and disciplinary assumptions. Endres (1996) states that nearly all CT theorists, either explicitly or implicitly, include this dimension in their models.

The ways in which knowledge is constructed are acknowledged in the **intellectual deliberations** dimension of CT. The **reflexive disposition** dimension of CT recognizes the potential strengths and shortcomings of any specific way of knowing and encourages consideration of other perspectives and other outcomes and consequences. The motivation and willingness to engage in intellectual deliberations and reflexive disposition come from **intellectual habits**. As students apply their growing capacity to engage CT in their course activities and assignments, they have opportunities to demonstrate each of the three dimensions of CT. Students can be expected to apply CT not only to the discussions and writing of others, but also to their own work.

Applying the Dimensions of CT to the Four Sample Activities

The following table demonstrates how the dimensions of CT that we have identified can be found in the four sample instructional activities. Not all three dimensions are represented in the simpler activities. The more extensive, multifaceted, and complex the instructional activity, the more opportunity students have to exhibit these three dimensions of CT in their practices.

Table 8
Example of the Dimensions Found in the Four Examples

Dimension	Chemistry Calibrated Peer Review (CPR)	Anthropology Role-Playing	History in Art Reflective Reading Report	Nursing Audio-Taped Interaction
Intellectual Habits	The variety of resources provided may stimulate intellectual curiosity for the problem presented. Intellectual curiosity would be reflected by students who go beyond resources provided to create stronger plans. Evaluation and justification of 3 peer essays and students' own essays against pre-established criteria require an intellectual work ethic for quality responses. Examples of calibrated essays and expectations of assignment set the standards to foster respect for evidence/reason.	Without clear guidelines on how to proceed, members will benefit if they tolerate ambiguity. A successful negotiation process requires the respectful interactions of willing collaborative inquiry, fair-mindedness in helping each other seek out and understand relevant perspectives toward a more effective solution, and open-mindedness to change if reasons to change are compelling.	The reflective reading report has potential to stimulate student intellectual curiosity and may enhance tolerance for the complexity of text ideas by inviting students to generate and discuss ideas, issues, and questions of personal interest or importance.	An effective interaction thrives under conditions that maximize fair-mindedness in striving to understand multiple, relevant perspectives and open-mindedness to change one's view if it leads to enhanced nurse-client interactions. An intellectual work ethic, intellectual curiosity, and collaborative inquiry may also be fostered as partners engage willingly in respectful collaboration as they explore experience, meaning, and outcomes that have direct implications for their chosen profession.
Intellectual deliberations	The CPR is based on the science model of inquiry. It is generally a structured inquiry where students formulate a plan but follow precise instructions. The students think scientifically and take responsibility for the process. They also must make and justify judgements about the quality of work for themselves and for their peers.	Role-playing a negotiation experience involving tribal conflict relies on observation and interpretation. Information about the history of the tribes is provided as background material. The dialogue between tribes is intended to produce an agreement or consensus about the best solution to the problem.	The reflective reading report is a type of literary criticism in that students analyze ideas in a piece of literature. Guiding questions provide an opportunity for students to read the text critically so that they can analyze and evaluate very simply what they have read.	The audiotaped interactions of a relational experience between nurse and client provide relevant background knowledge. Questions and examples that reflect relevant criteria guide deliberations throughout the inquiry process as partners engage in focused listening and share their thoughts and experiences. The outcomes of enhanced relational responsiveness inspire students to reflexively consider the adequacy of their knowledge and the effectiveness of their actions in a concrete situation.
Reflexive disposition	Guiding questions are provided to ensure students are clear about relevant criteria to guide their work. Repeated opportunities to analyse how calibrated samples reflect levels of success, to get feedback about judgements throughout related deliberations and reflections, to evaluate and justify peer essays, and to then evaluate and justify their own essays, allow students to revisit their interpretations and judgements toward more sustainable decisions.	Students learn during negotiations and debriefing that a satisfactory solution may look very different to other team members and tribes. As students' understanding of the connection between relevant perspectives and successful resolution to the conflict evolves, they may be more likely to generate negotiation strategies that are increasingly responsive to the needs of all participants.	The debriefing session allows students to hear other student responses to the same questions. This process leads them to understand that students may vary in their identification of what is salient or important to the issue at hand.	The assignment process supports students to look for the congruence between their espoused values, beliefs and actions and the values, beliefs and knowledge they actually enact in their work. As contradictions are revealed, students have the opportunity to identify and reshape the habits of mind and action that may be constraining their relational responsiveness and effectiveness in health care situations.

Using the Definition and Dimensions in the Instructional Process

Once the definition and dimensions of CT are explicit, teachers can draw on them in several ways to help with instructional planning and to communicate expectations to students.

1. Dimensions influence the design or choice of an instructional strategy and the resources and support students require. Some questions for consideration might include:

    i.   Are there opportunities in the assignment or class activity for students to demonstrate various **intellectual habits?** How?
    ii. What instruction and resources should be available for students to understand these required **intellectual habits** and their application to all their university work?
    iii. Does the activity provide opportunities for students to implement the **intellectual deliberations** of the area of study? Which ones?
    iv. Do the students need instruction and resources to understand and gain the competency to use **intellectual deliberations**?
    v.   Are there opportunities in the activity for students to demonstrate a **reflexive disposition?** How?
    vi. Do the students need instruction and resources to understand and gain the competency to demonstrate a **reflexive disposition**?

Figure 3 below illustrates the relationships among these aspects of teaching for CT.

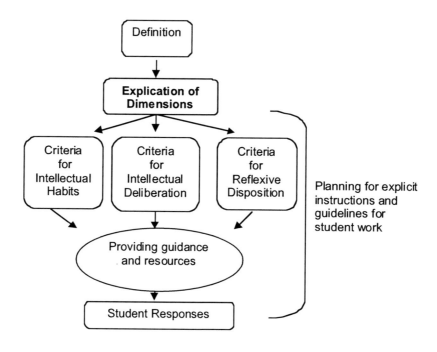

Figure 3.   Relationship of CT definition, dimensions, and criteria to instructional planning and guidance for students.

2. Each dimension includes a number of characteristics that instructors can use to assess whether students are engaging in CT. Instructors should specify the dimension and the main characteristics of the dimension they want students to be able to demonstrate, as well as the criteria or descriptors of the successful demonstration of these characteristics. Students can then learn explicitly *about* CT and demonstrate their competence in CT in their practices. It is important that instructors be able to apply this process to the three dimensions: intellectual habits, intellectual deliberation, and reflexive disposition.

   Organized activities should both require the students to demonstrate their understanding of CT and enable them to learn how to engage in CT through instruction and practice. Both the explication and the application are necessary components of learning CT as specific skills and general orientation.

3. The dimensions which characterize CT also provide the basis for how to assess and evaluate CT. As indicated previously, criteria for judging student success in the understanding and practice of the various characteristics of the CT dimensions must be included. Levels or standards of attainment for those criteria should also be specified by defining what constitutes an excellent, an average, or a poor standard for the various characteristics of each of the three dimensions (intellectual habits, intellectual deliberations, and reflexive disposition).

Figure 4 (see page 34) represents graphically the relationship between the criteria and standards for the dimensions of CT. It also demonstrates how to plan CT instruction, how to give guidance to students about expectations regarding CT, how to develop methods of assessment for CT and, finally, how to evaluate CT.

As we have already suggested, clarification of CT dimensions help guide students in course activities, provide them with knowledge for engaging in self-assessment, and enable them to reflect on their progress such that they will know in which area to seek help. Understanding these dimensions, their criteria, and how these can be demonstrated in practice can provide students with a foundation for thinking about and engaging in self-directed life-long learning.

Definitions, dimensions, and criteria should be provided to the students in writing so that requirements are clearly and easily available for discussion and further explanation. These can then be linked to the explicit criteria for success and to the CT learning outcomes set for the course. Chickering and Gamson (1987) state that good practice in undergraduate education includes setting high standards and this is one way that this practice can be achieved. Criteria and learning outcomes in teaching for CT are integral to setting such standards and will be addressed in the next section.

Figure 4. Relationship of CT definition, dimensions, criteria, and standards to instructional planning, guidance for students, and the assessment and evaluation of student work.

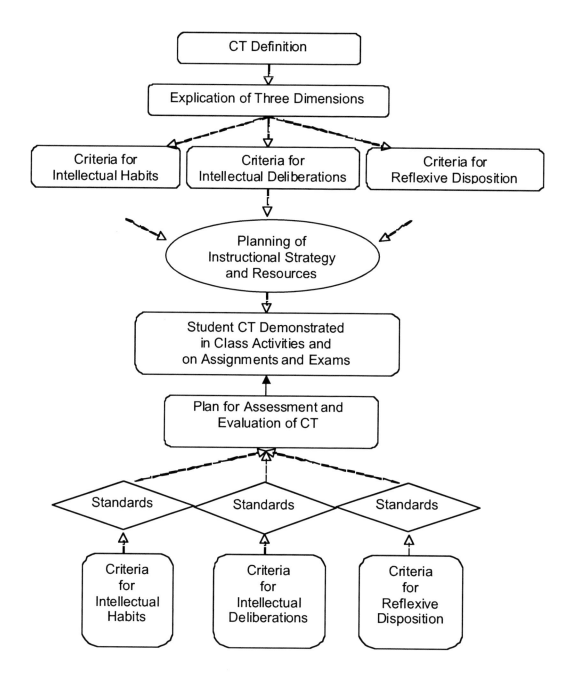

Critical Thinking Criteria and Related Learning Outcomes

'Would you tell me, please, which way I ought to go from here?" said Alice.
'That depends a good deal on where you want to get to,' said the Cat.
'I don't much care where,' said Alice.
'Then it doesn't matter which way you go,' said the Cat.

Lewis Carroll. *Alice in Wonderland.*

Criteria for the Dimensions of Critical Thinking

Criteria are descriptors of the desired components and qualities associated with CT. They are also relevant indicators for judging whether students are successfully engaging in CT. These criteria will help to clearly articulate expected CT learning outcomes. Criteria also provide the basis for assessment, since they allow for comparison and accountability of related judgements (Lipman, 1988). Standards, on the other hand, provide the basis for measuring the extent to which a criterion is in evidence (Case, 1997b) and ways that students' competence in the understanding and practice of CT can be evaluated.

The process of defining criteria, like that of developing clear formulations of definitions and dimensions, is essential because these explicit but generic descriptors of CT dimensions can be used in the design of all instructional activities. Although designing criteria is a substantial task and occasional review is necessary, the main design and much of the work only have to be done once. Table 9 provides the planning steps we have taken so far in making explicit the key elements involved in incorporating teaching for CT into courses and the relationship of criteria to these steps.

Table 9
Review of planning steps and their relationship to criteria for demonstrating student success in knowledge and practices of CT

Define CT in relation to your field of study	A quality of thinking that is characterized by *self-regulated use of intellectual habits and deliberations* on a challenge situation or task that involves *consideration of generated or selected alternatives, and culminates in making evaluative judgements. These judgements are based on criteria*, which *provide justifications* for the conclusion, and are applied to meaning, relational, empirical or value claims.		
Decide on and make explicit the categories of knowledge, skills, and values that will be displayed by an ideal Critical Thinker and illustrate the complexity of CT	Intellectual Habits	Someone who uses intellectual habits demonstrates: • Intellectual curiosity • Respect for truth and reason • Fair and open mindedness • Tolerance for ambiguity and complexity • Intellectual courage to take a position • Intellectual work ethic, and • Willingness to engage in collaborative inquiry.	Students will ask: What are the descriptors for each of these characteristics and what evidence must I give to indicate that I am using any or all of these characteristics?
	Intellectual Deliberations	Someone who engages in intellectual deliberations will: • Identify the challenge situation or task • Gather, interpret, and understand background information and other evidence • Apply thinking strategies relevant to the type of inquiry relevant to the challenge • Generate or select alternatives • Make evaluative judgements among alternatives based on criteria • Provide justification for the conclusion.	Students will ask: What evidence must I give to indicate that I have met the requirements of each of these aspects of inquiry?
	Reflexive Disposition (self-regulated)	Someone who exhibits a reflexive disposition will: • Plan ahead for CT • Monitor its quality throughout • Reflect on the strengths and limitations of the use of intellectual habits and intellectual deliberations in making a judgement.	Students will ask: What evidence must I give that I am exhibiting each or any of these characteristics?

We have found that developing generic criteria provides a reference point for creating the specific criteria that we would like to see students demonstrate in a particular class activity or assignment.

Case (1997b) suggests that criteria can take two forms:

1. Criteria that indicate empirically observable elements that should be included in the student response to the instructional activity, e.g.,
   Students will include both supportive and non-supportive evidence in coming to a decision.

2. Criteria that indicate the quality of the response, e.g.,
   Students will be able to articulate reasons that are relevant and sufficient to support their decision.

The instructor's particular approach to an area of study is exemplified in the use made of these criteria.

Tables 10, 11, 12 and 13 contain generic criteria chosen for each of the characteristics included in the dimensions of intellectual habits, intellectual deliberations, and reflexive disposition. We have also included the criteria for the different kinds of judgements that students may have to make. The criteria we use are based on descriptions that have significant support in the CT literature. We have purposefully worded them so that they are not aligned with any particular mode of inquiry and are not specific to any course activity or assignment.

1. Criteria for Intellectual Habits

We have described the quality of each of the intellectual habits that might be demonstrated by students. Obviously, not all CT activities will allow students to demonstrate the full range of habits. Thus, the instructors will identify the particular intellectual habits that they are stressing in the activity of their choice. These are contained in Table 10.

Table 10
Criteria for Intellectual Habits

Intellectual curiosity	Respect for truth and reason	Fair-minded	Open-minded	Tolerance for ambiguity and complexity	Intellectual courage to take a position	Intellectual work ethic	Willingness to engage in collaborative inquiry
Goes beyond readily available information to locate and use other relevant information toward more sustainable conclusions Pursues own curiosity about range of issues Seeks out opportunities for CT	Seeks most sustainable judgement Seeks out and uses relevant, sufficient reasons/evidence to support position Explicit about how some positions fit better with relevant criteria than other options Articulates sustainable case for the relative merit of support for a range of positions	Seeks out and represents strongest and weakest positions for both own and alternative position(s) Realistically weighs the pros and cons of implications of each option as they pertain to relevant perspectives Conclusion clearly represents an option that would be acceptable to those impacted by outcome of judgement Justification clearly shows why option chosen should be more acceptable than other options to relevant parties	If evidence/reasons uncovered during inquiry are more warranted than one's current position, one willingly changes one's position	Patient with and explicit about ideas that are evolving Makes explicit the limitations of one's current understanding Qualifies conclusions to show the evolving nature of support	Takes a position, even if unpopular, if one thinks it is more defensible than other positions or the morally right thing to do	Perseveres to do best, even when faces with unexpected challenges—does not give up Aims for systematicity and precision congruent with the nature of the situation or challenge	Respectful interactions; sensitive to differing levels of knowledge Responsible to fulfill one's role Helps others in group for the benefit of the quality of outcomes Seeks out opportunities for collaborative inquiry to come to a more sustainable conclusion

2. Criteria for Intellectual Deliberations

Table 11 contains the criteria that we have chosen for the four main characteristics of the intellectual deliberations dimension. Note that the criteria for making a judgement and justifying it are particular to the type of judgement being made. The criteria for each of those particular judgements are included in Table 12.

Table 11
Criteria for Student Demonstration of Intellectual Deliberations

Identifying the situation in need of CT judgement(s)	Gathering and interpreting background information	Selecting and using inquiry thinking strategies	Generate/select alternatives	Judging and Justifying
Plausible/accurate identification of the challenge situation or task in need of CT judgement(s)	Selection/use of information relevant and sufficient for the context of the challenge situation or task to progress towards sustainable judgements Accurate or plausible interpretation of background information	Selection of inquiry thinking strategies that effectively contribute to a sustainable judgement Effective use of inquiry thinking strategies Provision of evidence that plausibly supports the relative effectiveness or benefit of using or not using an inquiry thinking strategy	Generate or select comprehensive range of alternatives Alternatives for what to believe are relevant and plausible Alternatives for what to do have the potential to be effective in realizing goal about what should be done	Selection of relevant criteria for judgement among alternatives Application of relevant criteria in a manner appropriate to the mode of inquiry Plausible justification that explicitly evaluates the quality of support for the conclusion and the strength of fit between the support and the concluding judgement; ideally would also provide plausible account of why summative judgement is more sustainable than other options at this time *See samples of criteria relevant to particular kinds of judgements in Table 12*

Table 12
Criteria Relevant to Four Kinds of Judgements

Empirical	Meaning	Relational	Value
Direct observations: accurate, plausible, comprehensive *Observation reports:* accurate, plausible, comprehensive; replicable--other observers report the same thing *Artifacts:* accurate descriptions; plausible inferences; inferences congruent with other reputable sources, tests *Sources:* Credible--opportunity to know, capacity to know, tools in good working order, reputation for reliability, alignment with other reputable sources; theoretical potential for replication	*Intent of messenger:* clarity for target audience *Interpretation of intent of message:* accurate; plausible *Meaning of concepts:* congruence of definition with accepted use by competent language users (with knowledge of relevant context); congruence of examples of concepts with key attributes of definition that all examples share whereas non-examples lack at least one key attribute	*Conceptual relations:* relevancy, sufficiency, coherence *Logical relations:* relevancy, sufficiency, coherence; quality of relationship among premises and between premises and conclusion--a matter of degree, valid, or sound	*Objects:* what is valued about object within a domain by accepted authorities *Ideas, which may include criteria themselves:* congruency and sufficiency with societal needs and wants *Action and plans for action:* effectiveness (will the plan work?) -acceptability to those impacted by judgement (is it fair and safe?) -efficient in costs in time, resources, and effort--(is it feasible?)

3. Criteria for a Reflexive Disposition

When exhibiting a **reflexive disposition**, students deliberately assess and reflect on the strengths and weaknesses of the particular intellectual deliberations they are using and on their use of intellectual habits. This dimension reflects "your thinking about your way of thinking" but in a way that goes far beyond the question "Am I doing this right?" This dimension raises such questions as:

> *Are the intellectual deliberations that I am using adequate?*
>
> *Will the outcome (an evaluative judgement) be sustainable?*
>
> *Have I been fair-minded in the choice of outcomes and have I disregarded positions because others may view them negatively?*
>
> *In my collaborations with others in making this judgement, have I given full consideration to their perspectives?*

Table 13 describes the criteria that we have chosen for the characteristics of this dimension.

Table 13
Criteria for Student Demonstration of the Reflexive Disposition Dimension

Planning Ahead	Monitoring Throughout	Reflecting Back
Plausible identification, evaluation, and justification for/against adjustments in plans to ensure:	Ongoing monitoring and plausible evaluation and justification for/against adjustments to ensure:	Plausible evaluation and justification for/against adjustments to ensure:
relevance and congruence in plans among intellectual deliberations (identifying, gathering, deliberating, and judging that adhere to relevant criteria), intellectual habits, the challenge situation or task, and the situation requiring critical judgement	relevance of challenge situation or task to actual situation in need of CT response	stronger congruency among the challenge situation or task, intellectual dispositions, intellectual habits, and the actual situation requiring a CT judgement
relevant and sufficient ideas represented as a check list or other graphic organizer to guide inquiry	relevant and sufficient intellectual deliberations (identifying, gathering, deliberating, and judging that adhere to relevant criteria) and intellectual habits that are congruent with challenge	more comprehensive planning and monitoring the quality of response to the challenge
relevance and sufficiency of the kind of information identified, the range of options for judgement	comprehensive attention to relevant considerations via use of checklist or other means to track progress	use of more relevant, sufficient, and reliable information/sources
relevance, sufficiency, and reliability of sources	relevant, sufficient, and reliable information/sources used	enhanced effectiveness of inquiry thinking strategies
congruency and potential effectiveness of inquiry thinking strategies	maximizing effectiveness of inquiry thinking strategies	enhanced quality of support for judgement—accuracy/plausibility, potential for replication, congruency of relationships, congruency of meaning with competent users of language, acceptability of judgements when the outcome impacts others (was it fair, safe, and feasible?)
congruence among kinds of judgements, evidence/reasons, and criteria	quality support--clarity, accurate/plausible, relevant, congruent, acceptable, feasible, sufficient, systematic	stronger congruency among evidence/ reasons, judgements, and criteria
fairness to and safety for those who might be impacted by implementation of the plan	strong congruence among judgements, support, and criteria	stronger congruency between conclusion and quality of support
adequacy of role allocations for potential to maximize use of resources and quality of response in collaborative situations	maximum potential effectiveness of individuals through informed allocation of roles, responsibilities, and use of resources	enhanced allocation of roles, use of resources, and quality of response via better use of resources in both individual and collaborative situations

Relevant criteria for student demonstration of reflexive disposition should minimally include the *explicit and honest* evaluation of the adequacy of the intellectual deliberations and habits used. In evaluating the quality of students' justifications for their reflections on their response to the critical challenge situation/task, we would consider evidence of success to include a credible account of the sufficiency of and congruence among intellectual habits, intellectual deliberations, and the judgement reached. Students would be expected to provide a compelling case for why the judgements they reached are more sustainable than other possible options.

Writing Critical Thinking Learning Outcomes

CT learning outcomes are statements of explicit expectations for CT as a result of an individual's experience in a course, a specific activity, or an assignment. CT learning outcomes not only describe the ways in which students demonstrate that they have learned to think critically but also what they have learned through the process. Typically these outcomes are determined by what the instructor judges is an aspect of CT that students should learn or strengthen. By specifying outcomes, instructors increase the likelihood of providing students with targeted support for purposeful work.

Ideally, learning outcomes are written for a specific course or course activity, drawing upon the definition, dimensions, and generic criteria for CT that have already been established. Although writing such learning outcomes is time consuming, we encourage instructors to take the time and make the additional effort to define CT, to decide what dimensions are associated with their definition, and to create general criteria for describing a successful demonstration of these dimensions before setting learning outcomes. The investment in time and effort is worthwhile.

The degree to which all of the learning outcomes are closely connected to the development of facility in the application of CT will, in large measure, determine to what extent students engage in making evaluative judgements. It is vital to ensure that students have the understanding and competencies to engage in making appropriate judgements. When teaching for CT becomes widespread, each learning outcome in a course might be expressed in terms of the dimensions of CT. The course content would then offer the necessary background information and specific disciplinary knowledge relevant to students making informed judgement in their learning activities.

Typically, learning outcomes state how students must demonstrate their intellectual understanding, skills, and values. When properly written, the outcomes will convey to learners exactly what is to be accomplished and provide instructors with direction in planning the content, instruction, and evaluation in the course.

Good learning outcomes specify some action that learners must produce in a manner that is observable and measurable. For this reason, all good CT learning outcomes have similar features. They state clearly the production of some of the dimensions of CT by the learners in a manner that is observable and measurable.

The following are the major CT learning outcomes associated with each of the sample CT activities described in Section 2. For each outcome we have indicated the dimensions of CT and the CT criteria that could best be demonstrated by students engaged in these activities.

Activity: Chemistry Calibrated Peer Review

LEARNING OUTCOME #1:
Students will be able to make informed judgements about the process by which the $Ag_2S(s)$ layer on silver coins could be converted back to $Ag(s)$ in an electrolytic cell and write a short essay indicating how and why they came to make these judgements.

MAIN CRITICAL THINKING DIMENSIONS

Criteria	INTELLECTUAL HABITS	INTELLECTUAL DELIBERATIONS	REFLEXIVE DISPOSITION
Specific characteristics (desired qualities/ parts) described	*Intellectual curiosity* Students supplement resources provided by actively seeking out additional resources that contribute to a more sustainable response. *Intellectual work ethic* Students persevere until they achieve expectations for accurate information relevant to an effective plan for removing silver sulfide from silver coins.	*Gather and interpret relevant background information* Students gather relevant, accurate, and sufficient information to formulate a plan that can successfully remove silver sulfide from silver coins. *Making judgements based on criteria and standards provided* Students are able to base judgements about a plan on relevant criteria—a plan that accurately, completely, and logically delineates an effective way to remove silver sulfide from silver coins.	*Plan, monitor, and reflect on quality of thinking throughout deliberations* Students re-read, re-think, and honestly and explicitly re-evaluate adequacy of intellectual habits and intellectual deliberations as they apply to use of resources, feedback, and content in own and peer essays as they strive throughout deliberations to improve the quality of responses and their congruence with the concluding judgements.

LEARNING OUTCOME #2:
Students will be able to critically evaluate short essays with respect to the quality of their content and writing style and critically reflect on their own capability for writing such essays.

MAIN CRITICAL THINKING DIMENSIONS

Criteria	INTELLECTUAL HABITS	INTELLECTUAL DELIBERATIONS	REFLEXIVE DISPOSITION
Criteria (desired qualities/ parts) described	*Intellectual work ethic* Students persevere as they demonstrate increasing congruence between their work and a competent standard of achievement. *Respect for reason* Students persevere to provide reasons that adequately support their judgements.	*Make judgements based on relevant criteria and standards* Students use guiding questions and 3 calibrated sample essays as they make plausible judgements about which standard of competence (beginning, developing, and competent) is most evident in their own and in peer essays. Criteria include accurate information, as well as a well-written, integrative paragraph with a descriptive topic sentence, no evidence of run-on sentences or sentence fragments, and correct spelling.	*Monitor and reflect on quality of thinking to improve thinking* Students use evidence from peer and own essays, readings, calibrated samples, and guiding questions/expectations as they revisit their work and increasingly strengthen the congruence between the standards, their evaluative marks, and the quality of their own essays.

Activity: Role-Play in Anthropology

LEARNING OUTCOME #1:
Students will be able to make an informed choice among all options that are offered to solve the tribal dispute and demonstrate fair-mindedness in that choice.

MAIN CRITICAL THINKING DIMENSIONS

Criteria	INTELLECTUAL HABITS	INTELLECTUAL DELIBERATIONS
Criteria (desired qualities/ parts) described	*Fair-mindedness* Students' deliberations and reflexive dispositions clearly demonstrate a desire to seek out and understand relevant perspectives and to reach sustainable outcomes, as they are most acceptable to those who may be affected by them. *Willingness to engage in collaborative inquiry* Students participate constructively in-role to help tribal members understand relevant tribal perspectives and to use this knowledge to develop strategies with strong potential to effectively resolve the tribal conflict.	*Gather and interpret relevant background information* Students strive to understand the information provided to comprehend its relevance to tribal perspectives (ways of being, needs, historical conflicts) in order to make informed decisions that have potential to resolve the conflict. *Generate alternatives and select criteria to guide judgements* As students work in role, they negotiate strategies that they think might work to resolve the conflict (criteria are implicit at this stage). *Make judgement based on relevant criteria* Students make plausible connections between what they have learned about cultural differences and needs with strategies that they think will be potentially effective to resolve the conflict over the use of land (criteria are still implicit).

LEARNING OUTCOME #2:
Students will provide a justification for the option chosen, indicating why the chosen option will resolve the tribal dispute better than the alternative options.

MAIN CRITICAL THINKING DIMENSIONS

Criteria	INTELLECTUAL HABITS	INTELLECTUAL DELIBERATIONS	REFLEXIVE DISPOSITION
Criteria (desired qualities/ parts) described	*Respect for truth and reason* Students demonstrate respect for truth in their honest and plausible account of the adequacy of their deliberations, applications of fair-mindedness, and collaborative decision-making. Students demonstrate respect for reason by reflecting on and justifying the sustainability of their judgements. *Intellectual work ethic* Students persevere until they arrive at a judgement that has plausible potential to resolve the conflict.	*Justify the judgement* Students explicitly and honestly provide a plausible evaluative account of the quality of deliberations and application of relevant habits of mind (fair-mindedness, willingness to engage in collaborative inquiry) in reaching their judgement. Students also provide a plausible evaluation of the strength of congruence between the quality of deliberations and habits of mind and the concluding judgement about a strategy to effectively negotiate a resolution to the tribal conflict. *Justify the relative merit of the judgement* Students are able to address relative merit by providing a plausible account of how fair-minded deliberations that respond to the needs of relevant perspectives are more likely to lead to an effective resolution than deliberations that do not respect the needs of some perspectives.	*Plan, monitor, and reflect on the quality of thinking to improve one's thinking* Students, guided by prompting questions from the instructor, make explicit the criteria that made possible an effective negotiation that resolved the conflict. For example, relevant criteria would likely include the need for fair-mindedness when deliberating toward comprehensive consideration of relevant cultural differences and needs, a range of options with potential to work, and a conclusion that would resolve the conflict as it takes into account the needs of both groups (i.e., is it safe, fair, and feasible?)

Activity: Art History Reflective Reading Report

Criteria	**LEARNING OUTCOME:** Students will be able to read analytically; that is, they will be able to identify and justify important ideas in the reading, identify issues that need further consideration or research, and pose questions they wish to pursue further. **MAIN CRITICAL THINKING DIMENSIONS**		
	INTELLECTUAL HABITS	**INTELLECTUAL DELIBERATIONS**	**REFLEXIVE DISPOSITION**
Criteria (desired qualities/ parts) described	*Intellectual curiosity* Students actively pursue own curiosity about range of issues/ideas in reading. *Tolerance for ambiguity and complexity* Students make explicit plausible limitations of their current understanding by generating questions congruent with their expressed need for further consideration or inquiry.	*Make judgements based on criteria relevant to kind of judgement required* Students judge which 3 ideas in a reading are most important to them. Ideas chosen represent a plausible fit with the meaning of important (e.g., it is plausible that what one believes or does about the idea has the potential to impact someone in significant way). *Justify fit between criteria and questions generated by students* Students make explicit, plausible connections between their choices and relevant criteria.	*Plan, monitor, and reflect on the quality of thinking to improve one's thinking* Students make plausible connections as they evaluate to what degree their own ideas fit the criterion of important or burning and as they consider the questions that need further inquiry.

Activity: Audiotaped Interaction in Nursing

Criteria	**LEARNING OUTCOME: #1** Students will be able to interpret and evaluate the congruence between their espoused theories of practice and their actual interactions in practice. **MAIN CRITICAL THINKING DIMENSIONS**		
	INTELLECTUAL HABITS	**INTELLECTUAL DELIBERATIONS**	**REFLEXIVE DISPOSITION**
Criteria (desired qualities/ parts) described	*Intellectual work ethic* Students persevere to do their best to plausibly represent interactions and changes to interactions.	*Selects and interprets and represents relevant background information* Students provide relevant, plausible and comprehensive representations of their interpretations of the nature of client-nurse interactions in each of the baseline and final audiotapes. Students provide plausible and comprehensive representations of their interpretations of change in quality of client-nurse interactions.	*Plan, monitor, and reflect on the quality of thinking to improve one's thinking* Students use analysis sheets to record a plausible evaluation of the quality of their interactions during and following the actual audiotaping.

LEARNING OUTCOME: #2

Students will be able to evaluate and revise the aspects of their practice that may be constraining their relational responsiveness and effectiveness in health care situations.

MAIN CRITICAL THINKING DIMENSIONS

Criteria	INTELLECTUAL HABITS	INTELLECTUAL DELIBERATIONS	REFLEXIVE DISPOSITION
Criteria (desired qualities/ parts) described	*Intellectual work ethic* Students persevere to do their best to represent interactions in plausible way. *Respect for truth/reason* Students show respect for truth in their explicit, honest, and plausible interpretations of the nature of client-nurse interactions. Students' representations of the interactions and changes to them are congruent with the degree desired qualities are present in the interactions.	*Select and interpret and represent relevant background information* Students provide relevant, comprehensive, clear, and plausible representation of the client-nurse interactions. *Apply criteria provided in guiding questions to judgements about the nature of relationships* Students provide plausible judgements about the strength of congruence between interactions and relational qualities such as empathy, initiation, responsiveness, authenticity, and so on. Students provide a plausible account of the degree of change in congruence between desired qualities and actual performance evident in the two audiotapes. *Justify congruence between judgements and relevant criteria* Students' plans for continued improvement of the desired qualities in client-nurse interactions and build, in a comprehensive way, on relevant insights about what did and did not work to construct plans that have a likely potential to enhance client-nurse interactions.	*Monitor and reflect on quality of thinking to improve thinking* Students' reflections on thoughts during the activity and after the activity are congruent with the quality of deliberations, habits of mind, and concluding judgements about the nature of client-nurse relationships. Students integrate these evaluative reflections in an honest and comprehensive way as they create plans that have plausible potential to enhance the quality of future client-nurse interactions.

Once instructors have established the overall definition of CT, spelled out its dimensions, articulated the general criteria for demonstrating these dimensions, and identified learning outcomes specific to the target course or course activity, they can now present a clear picture of what and how they expect students to learn. Instructors can be explicit and detailed with students about what their expectations are for them in the course both for what the course content will be and for how students will be enabled to develop an understanding of and facility in CT through course activities.

Instructional Strategies to Facilitate Critical Thinking

High-quality learning leading to the attainment of conceptual understanding, higher-order cognitive and metacognitive skills, and self-regulated learning is meaning-directed, application-directed and self-directed in nature, many times also involving student collaboration in small groups.

Vermunt (2003), p. 121.

Features of Critical Thinking Instructional Strategies

Effective instructional strategies to support teaching for CT are learning-centred, involving more than "covering" content and transmitting information. Actively engaged instructors show students, both in their discourse and their pedagogy, that course content consists of well-developed scholarly positions that have been reached through rigorous inquiry and CT associated with inquiry in the field (see for example, R. Paul, *Foundation for Critical Thinking*, 2004. http://www.criticalthinking.org).

Since knowledge is constantly developing in all disciplines, students must be encouraged to take on the same dialogic stance as their instructors when engaging new problems, new arguments, and new evidence. Instructors should model such a dialogic stance in engaging their disciplinary subject matter and interacting with students. In teaching for CT, as with all active learning strategies, instructors take on facilitating, guiding, and prompting roles. They not only act as expert resources, but also as models of inquiry and sources of feedback. One of the most important roles instructors play is designing the learning environment such that CT is promoted and supported in the learning activities *per se*.

Effective CT instructional strategies are characterized by the following three features:

1. A critical challenge that creates an impetus for learning content and invites varied responses.

2. Time for students to think and reflect on the critical challenge before producing a response, followed by time both to reflect on that response and to make revisions.

3. Collegial interactions involving student and instructor, and student and peers.

The Critical Challenge

CT occurs when the learner is faced with or confronted by occasions of ambiguity or uncertainty. Case and Wright (1997) call such an occasion a critical challenge and Brookfield (1987) refers to it as a critical trigger. Elements of uncertainty and ambiguity can be imbedded in various aspects of the challenge such as in the representation of a central problem or issue, definitions of concepts, quality of available evidence and reasons, necessity for alternate solutions, competing priorities, and competing values. Instructional strategies that elicit CT, therefore, are ones that present students with an intellectual challenge, in response to which they have to make a judgement (empirical, meaning, relational, or value) of some kind (scientific, legal, aesthetic, ethical or other). In this way, instructional strategies designed to elicit CT can also motivate students to understand and to draw on course content to address and revolve the critical challenge.

A critical challenge is made up of a source for the challenge – what the student is going to think critically about – and a frame – the instructions guiding the student to think critically (generally described in the form of a question or task). For example, in the reflective reading activity described in Section 2, the source of the challenge is the reading and the frame is created by the three questions. In the anthropology role-play, the source for the challenge is background material on each of the tribes and the frame is the instruction to solve the tribal conflict through negotiation. In the chemistry calibrated peer review example, one source for a critical challenge is the writing assignments of other students in the class and the frame is provided by the requirement to give criteria-based feedback on the assignments. The source for the critical challenge in the fourth year nursing example is the audiotaped interactions between the client and practitioner and the frame is provided by the guiding questions.

The critical challenge, as a necessary condition for eliciting CT, ideally has the following seven characteristics (adapted from Case & Wright, 1997; Ford, 1998):

1. It is meaningful to students in that it connects to previous learning and understanding or reconciles their prior knowledge with new information.

2. It is relevant to course learning outcomes.

3. It addresses significant or provocative problems, circumstances, or issues in the area of study.

4. It presents some uncertainty that must be resolved.

5. It requires the application of specific intellectual resources that students currently possess or can acquire in the process of responding to the challenge.

6. It requires adequate resources to support students in responding to the critical challenge so that most of the time and effort necessary to make considered and informed judgements can be applied to the intellectual task rather than to organizational tasks.

7. Ultimately, it requires evaluative judgements about proposed meaning, relationships, or the interactions among propositions, explanatory or empirical claims, and value or worth.

Whether designing a short in-class activity to elicit CT or designing an entire course fully incorporating CT, the critical challenge should be characterized by these seven features. Table 14 indicates how each of the four sample activities which are integral to instructional strategies of the four courses is congruent with the seven characteristics necessary to a critical challenge.

Table 14

Congruence Between Sample Activities and Characteristics of a Critical Challenge

Criteria for Critical Challenge	Chemistry	Anthropology	History in Art	Nursing
Critical challenge: The frame	Create a plan for cleaning silver sulfide from coins. Evaluate congruence of plans with calibrated essays.	Decide how to resolve conflict between two tribes about the use of land.	Decide on three issues worth remembering, two issues for follow-up inquiry, and one burning question.	Evaluate practitioner effectiveness. Develop plan to enhance practitioner-client interactions.
Critical challenge: The source The critical challenge source is meaningful to the student in that it connects to previous learning and understanding or reconciles their prior knowledge with new information.	Students will require relevant experiences, concepts and other ideas foundational to this topic and task. They are provided with relevant resources and encouraged to go beyond them as needed to construct and evaluate plans.	Students are provided a handout with instructions for the task and relevant background information about the different norms and customs of the tribes people.	Generic questions allow students to connect to issues, ideas, and questions in the text that are significant to them.	Students create their own audiotape of client-practitioner interactions for analysis. They are provided with questions and an analysis sheet with sample responses and criteria to guide observations, reflections and judgements.
The critical challenge is relevant to course learning outcomes.	By responding to the challenge, students should be able to demonstrate understanding of relevant scientific reactions, states, principles and electron transfer. By evaluating their own and peer plans, against calibrated samples, students should be able to demonstrate increasing competency in judging quality of essays.	Through the role-play and judgement to resolve the conflict, students should be able to demonstrate understanding of the important role of social and cultural factors when dealing with conflict.	By responding to generic questions, students should be able to demonstrate understanding of course content.	By analyzing and reflecting on audiotape interactions, student nurses should be able to demonstrate more informed judgements about effective practitioner-client relationships.
The critical challenge addresses significant or provocative problems, circumstances or issues in the area of study.	Students will be motivated by the simulation of the application of their knowledge about chemical reactions.	Understanding cultural diversity related to socially responsible judgements and actions is a complex activity and multiple responses are expected.	Students will likely be more inspired toward understanding text content by responding to generic questions/tasks that prompt personal connections to and reflections on the content.	Nurses do more in their profession than provide medical guidance and assistance. They also experience emotional connections with their clients.

The critical challenge requires activities that allow students to apply developing or existing understandings of CT dimensions (intellectual habits, intellectual deliberations, and reflexive disposition) or activities that include teaching relevant CT dimensions so that students may respond successfully to the challenge.	Students access a variety of resources for background knowledge for the assignment. Students are provided with explicit criteria and three calibrated sample essays representing standards for three levels of attainment. These criteria and samples, along with instructor feedback, are used to guide students' evaluative judgements with supporting justifications of peer essays and their own essays.	Students have opportunity to interpret other points of view toward fair-mindedness as they represent in-role one of two cultural groups and deliberate collaboratively toward an effective solution to the conflict. They are provided with information about relevant cultural and social norms that must be addressed if deliberations are to lead to an effective resolution of the conflict.	As they read the text, students interpret meaning, reflect on ideas, and make evaluative judgements about which ideas have personal significance and which ideas warrant further personal inquiry; the provocative nature of ideas facilitate intellectual curiosity about different views about art history.	Students are provided with questions, an example, and qualities of interactions to interpret and guide their client-practitioner relationship and reflections on the nature of the interactions. The challenge situation supports intellectual habits of demonstrating respect and sensitivity for others, as well as honouring complexity and ambiguity.
The critical challenge requires that students have adequate resources (materials, time, understanding) to make informed judgements.	Students are provided with relevant content resources, calibrated samples, and are also encouraged to seek additional resources for their assignment. Feedback is given to students for their peer reviews.	Students are given handouts with the instructions for the role-play as well as background information on the tribes. Throughout the exercise, the professor circulates to monitor student thinking by asking a variety of questions.	Students have required text readings and the professor provides the questions for the reflective reading.	Students have access to resources including instructions with example, the time to complete the tasks, and assistance from the professor as needed.
The challenge requires evaluative judgements.	Students judge three peer essays based on pre-established criteria for low, mid and high quality essays and also judge the quality of their own work.	Students negotiate a judgement to resolve a conflict between two tribes.	Students judge which three ideas in the text are worth remembering and which ideas require further inquiry.	Students judge the effectiveness of their client-practitioner relationships and use this knowledge to inform future practice.

Time for Reflection

At all stages of the CT process, time for reflection is important. The length of time varies with the degree of complexity, from a critical question posed in class and allotted a relatively short time for reflection to a literary critique requiring a considerably longer time for reflection. Students should be encouraged to reflect without feeling rushed to provide an immediate answer, since by rushing they may miss evidence, points of view, or new interpretations. Developing this intellectual habit of taking time to reflect is a gradual process. Instructors can encourage such intellectual patience by rewarding careful deliberations and cautious conclusions. While students should be encouraged to suspend judgement or delay coming to a definitive answer too quickly, this systematic pausing can create difficulties since many students expect an immediate 'right answer' and dislike experiencing a state of uncertainty.

Collegial Interaction: Student and Instructor and Student and Student

When teaching for CT is central, class time is devoted to discussion and other interactive or engaging activities. Little time is taken up by the style of lecturing that sees covering the course content as a primary objective (see Brookfield, 1987; Gokhale, 1995; Vygotsky, 1978; Anderson [as cited in Bruffee, 1999]).

Collaboration among students can produce increased analysis and synthesis of evidence and background information, leading to critical evaluation through argumentation and developing of consensus. A collaborative environment encourages students to be more reflective in their answers, to provide reasons for their judgements, and to consider and make explicit the criteria upon which they arrive at these judgements.

One of the major obstacles to designing teaching for CT is the tension between the need to cover course content and the time required, both in and out of the scheduled class time, for students to reflect and interact in order to learn through CT. The tension between learning content and opportunities for CT can be reduced if instructional methods that encourage learning of content through CT activities are chosen (see Case, 1997a). Learning content through CT ensures that students gain the knowledge that is necessary in any particular area. In lower level courses, the acquisition of vast foundational content is considered critical for future success. Typically, it is in these courses that there is resistance to an overall strategy of student-centred learning. However, the "working the content" approach using CT that we advocate has received significant support (Fox & Hackerman, 2003) and is congruent with contemporary theories of learning (Bransford et al., 2000). Such an approach bridges the supposed dichotomy between either covering content or developing CT.

Individual instructor approaches to choice of content are best understood when they ask themselves questions like the following:

1. What knowledge should students acquire and integrate with their previous knowledge?

2. What meaningful application resulting in an evaluative judgement would require that knowledge? Meaningful applications may include decision-making, problem solving, engaging in inquiry, inventing, creating, etc.

3. What kind of intellectual deliberations will students be using in this activity?

A series of questions to guide students through to making those formative judgements can be prepared. Here are some examples of questions.

- Compare and contrast the theories of X, Y, and Z, and determine which appears to have the most support in the current literature cited. Which has the least support? Why?

- What do these three theories have in common? Is the common element a critical feature of all three?

- If you were to construct an argument for the position of Y in addressing the problem, what evidence would you use to support your position?

- How would you refute the evidence that does not support this position?

- Are all of these theories based on the same assumptions?

- Should any of the assumptions not articulated be examined?

- Are there potential consequences of the application of any or all of these theoretical approaches that make application ill-advised?

- What criteria would be relevant in the evaluation of the three theoretical alternatives?

As students practice learning by using this approach, the guiding questions may remain important only to help the instructor in doing assessment.

The above approach is based on two premises. First, if students see relevance and meaning in their learning, they are more motivated to apply intellectual effort to the process, which results in *deep* rather than *surface* learning (Biggs, 1987; 1993; Entwistle, 1981; Ramsden, 2003). Second, through "working the content" (Case, 1997, p. 143), students can acquire content and practice the application of accepted intellectual deliberations of inquiry.

Table 15 describes how each of the four examples has been designed to engage students in CT and to ensure that they acquire and integrate new knowledge within the context of the previous experience and understanding.

Table 15

Learning Content through Critical Thinking: Application to the Four Examples

Questions to ask	Chemistry	Anthropology	History in Art	Nursing
What knowledge do I want students to acquire and integrate with their previous knowledge?	Students interpret a number of resources about chemical reactions that contribute to the formation of silver sulfide and ideas to help them formulate a plan to electro-chemically remove the layer of silver sulfide from a silver object.	Students review social and cultural background information to acquire an understanding of two tribes and their conflicting needs for use of the land. They integrate this knowledge as they brainstorm solutions to the impasse.	Students read a text to develop familiarity with contemporary art-historical theory and integrate ideas and issues with personal priorities and interests.	Students share personally challenging experiences with a partner who responds to them. These interactions are audio-taped to provide background information to help partners acquire an understanding of relational responses and integrate their understanding in order to be an effective nurse.
What kind of deliberations will students be using in this activity, recognizing that not all will be applicable?	Students interpret resource information and refine their understanding as they develop a plan to restore coins and as they interpret and evaluate peer essays for congruence with the calibrated models.	If the impasse is to be resolved, students will need to respond to the challenge situation by interpreting through observation and interaction in-role the cultural patterns and context of the two tribes in order to test options for acceptability to each group.	Students interpret ideas in art history text, evaluate which alternatives are personal priorities/ interests, and then share and justify their choices.	Students refine their relational skills as they interpret and critically reflect on their interactions with the client. Focus questions help them to critically analyze the 2 tapes.
What meaningful application that results in an evaluative judgement would require that information?	Knowledge of scientific reactions, states, and principles is used to help students judge the standard of achievement of essays about plans for silver sulfide removal.	Knowledge of patterns of cultural norms and context is used to role-play tribal responses to the challenge situation to come to judgement about which negotiation strategy is most acceptable to both tribes.	Knowledge of information in selected history of art text is required if students are to be able to evaluate, share, and justify which ideas are personally more important, interesting, and/or worthy of further inquiry.	Knowledge of qualities of nurse-client relationships guide judgement and reflection toward effective interactions.

Categories of Instructional Strategies that Elicit Critical Thinking

An instructional strategy is an educational plan of action that is implemented with the intention of accomplishing a specific learning goal. Instructors must choose or design activities and assignments that will engage the student with the course content and facilitate their understanding of this content. To develop CT, the instructional strategy should include a *critical challenge, time for reflection and collegial interaction*. Generally, lecturing does not prove effective for the latter two features. Instructors should focus on those activities that could: (a) be implemented in lieu of lecturing or (b) be used to punctuate a lecture. Note that all suggested categories of instructional strategies focus on student activity. The instructional strategies advocated here are consistent with a commitment to engaging students in the classroom and having them work the content of the course.

None of the general categories of instructional strategies mentioned briefly in this section are new. They are all used widely and their merits and techniques have been explained extensively in other resources. Therefore we will mention these instructional strategies very briefly in the context of teaching for CT. More detailed descriptions can be found in sources listed in the References.

The general categories of instructional strategies that we have included in this section involve conversing, writing, and experiencing. Students learn through talking about, writing about, and experiencing the processes and concepts integral to a course.

Conversing

Intellectual conversations help to develop critical thinking. Three general forms are discussion, dialectical conversation, and dialogical conversation. A *discussion* is the most informal of these categories and involves an exchange of ideas or perspectives among individuals, with the goal of revealing and understanding core values and the assumptions that underpin these values. Two related forms are *dialectical and dialogical conversation.* Despite similarities of name they are different. *Dialectical conversation* develops logical arguments to construct support for a particular position, using debate with those who hold opposing views. *Dialogical conversation* has the goal of transforming perspectives and constructing shared meaning through reflection and consensus building with others who hold different views.

In all forms of conversation, there should be an emphasis on active listening and on attaining a higher level of understanding among the discussants. Furthering understanding is achieved through challenging ideas and perspectives or by raising questions about ideas and perspectives.

Conversation may also take place by electronic means, which provide creative ways of ensuring collegial interaction for CT in large classes. There is some evidence that electronic conversations can support critical thinking as effectively, and in some cases, more effectively than in face-to-face conditions, since, at least in asynchronous electronic messaging there can be more time for thought and reflection (Collison, Elbaum, Haavind, & Tinker, 2000; Sloffer, Dueber, & Duffy, 1999).

Several conditions are necessary for conversations to engage in CT: (a) instructors must have a specific outcome or a particular purpose in mind for the discussion; (b) students must be well prepared for discussion; and, (c) ground rules should be developed to ensure that the interaction is collegial. It is critical that various perspectives be included and that each and every member of the class be heard.

Critical Challenges for Conversing

There are a countless number of sources for critical challenges for conversing including readings, case studies, current events, guest lectures, problems, contradictory student viewpoints on course concepts, and research findings, to identify only a few. The challenge frame, generally posed in the form of questions, must create some controversy that invites multiple responses or the process stalls. These questions must be open-ended and sufficiently substantial so that the conversation can evolve. The questions should generate some uncertainty for the discussants, thus requiring them to deliberate on the issues associated with the challenge source. Collison et al. (2000) distinguish between questions that serve to gather evidence (Who? What? When? Where? Why?) and questions that provide opportunities to scrutinize both one's own and other's perspectives and values, and that promote deeper understanding. The authors refer to these latter forms of questions as full-spectrum questioning strategies that prompt discussants to:

- Query the relevance of the source of the critical challenge to different constituents under varying conditions (e.g., Why is this particular issue worth considering?)

- Make clear the meaning of the terms or concepts related to the critical challenge (e.g., Could you clarify what you mean when you use that terminology? Is that term useful in this situation?)

- Probe for assumptions and the sources of those assumptions in the critical challenge and in one's own thinking (e.g., It appears that most of you agree with the commonly held position but is there any validity to the opposing position?)

- Search for relationships or connections (e.g., You have identified several factors that appear to precede the outcome. What type of relationship might each of these factors have to the result? To each other?)

- Make evaluative judgements that will inform a plan of action (e.g., What are the consequences of this evidence? How will you proceed? What is your position now?)

- Reflect on the plan of action or your conclusion in terms of its plausibility, relevance to stakeholders, and sustainability (What is the strength of this plan? What is your conclusion? Given the context, is it feasible to take this position?)

Time for Reflection

The critical challenge to students should be provided well before the conversation is to take place so that students can reflect on it and be prepared to participate (Bean, 1996). Discussion is aided by writing exercises, such as the reflective reading report strategy described earlier, or a requirement that students generate questions that can be addressed in a class discussion.

In an electronic environment with asynchronous conferencing tools, students have more time to reflect, not only on their own input, but also on the input of others. Since this type of conversing crosses the boundary into writing activities, students should be encouraged to think carefully about and engage in revisions of their written responses.

Collegial Interaction

Conversation is one of the primary ways in which instructors can interact with students and in which students can interact with each other. To ensure successful interaction, the instructor needs to act as a moderator, willing to engage in the conversation in three ways (Collison et al., 2000):

1. Sharpening the focus of the discussion by: (a) identifying the direction of the discussion; (b) encouraging discussants to classify ideas for their relevance to the goal of the discussion; and (c) encouraging discussants to focus on the critical points.

2. Encouraging the deepening of the discussion and coaching CT through: (a) using a wide spectrum of question types; (b) encouraging discussants to identify and make connections among concepts; and (c) identifying and including alternative perspectives.

3. Modelling CT through: (a) clarifying assumptions and indicating how these influence perspective; (b) challenging the validity of a common or standard belief, value or position in order to support discussants in uncovering alternatives; and (c) suspending judgement of discussants' positions and continually seeking clarification or justification for their positions.

Students need to know that the classroom is a place in which their views will be welcomed. Before undertaking any form of open conversation, a class discussion should be held in which the nature of good conversations, the behaviour of participants, and the role of the moderator are clarified. Such a discussion will encourage CT and the participation of all. From such a discussion, instructors and students can generate a set of criteria. When subsequent conversations fail, the class is able to reflect on the criteria to determine if any were violated or if any revisions are necessary.

Conversation Formats

Among the many conversation formats are the following: large group format, small group format, think-pair-share activities, peer instruction (Mazur, 1997), pyramidal discussion, fish bowl, jigsaw, panel discussion, and open debate in teams.

Writing

Writing activities can challenge students to learn to engage in CT, but like other instructional formats, a critical challenge, time to reflect, and collegial interaction are necessary features for teaching for CT to be effective.

The academic writing process provides the opportunity for students to clarify meaning, to identify connections, to construct and reconstruct an argument, and to make their perspectives explicit to themselves and then to others. The CPR example provided earlier employs such exploratory writing.

Writing activities requiring higher-level intellectual skills are integrated into courses to ensure that content is assessed and revised. These contribute significantly to teaching for CT. Although the classic 'term paper' is central to many courses, too frequently it does not provide for rethinking, revision, and resubmission. To be effective the "term paper" should be structured into sequences of research, annotated bibliography, thesis statement, outline, first draft, second draft, etc. Instructors who wish to strengthen their students' engagement in CT should consider structuring this approach into their essay writing requirements.

Writing strategies can be categorized as *informal or formative* and *formal or summative*. Exploratory writing, informal or formative writing focuses on students' thinking. Such writing activities range from short "in the moment" writing assignments in which students write to clarify their ideas in class through to reflective journals in which students track their understanding and comment on their practice or progress kept throughout a course.

As a writing strategy, formal or summative writing allows instructors to determine whether and to what extent students have understood the course content, are able to engage in CT, and are able to write in a manner appropriate to the area of study. Examples of formal writing include expository, persuasive, or literary essays, evaluative or review essays, research reports, and literature reviews.

Formative, exploratory writing activities provide significant opportunities for students to learn to engage in CT since such activities can be employed frequently in a course. A variety of opportunities to engage in formative writing improves the quality of summative writing both in the formal structure of the writing and use of critical thinking (Elbow, 1997). Both the reflective writing report in History in Art and the CPR activity in Chemistry are good examples of exploratory writing.

Formal writing assignments provide the best opportunities for instructors to assess critical thinking (Ennis & Weir, 1985) and are usually undertaken individually. The most effective and productive CT writing instructional activities allow for both informal and formal writing production.

Critical Challenges for Writing

Like discussions, there are many writing activity sources for effective critical challenges, including personal experience, readings, specific course content, student presentations or writing, and current events related to the course topics. The directions or questions that form the frame for the critical challenge are crucial to the degree of engagement in critical thinking. Providing topics for writing activity directs student writers to the source for a critical challenge but does not provide a critical frame for their engagement. Full spectrum questions reviewed in the previous section apply here as in discussions. Another possible frame for the critical challenge can be derived from the particular intellectual deliberations that students are to employ. This would include statements that direct students to compare and contrast, analyze, synthesize, analyze errors, or analyze perspectives about ideas or concepts leading to an evaluative judgement. Using the frame can also encourage identification and evaluation of relevant sources, interpretation and organization of information, selection of effective thinking strategies, and the generation and evaluation of alternatives.

Another strategy for encouraging CT which produces the frame for a source at the same time is requiring students to develop a critical question in relationship to the source material. From such a frame, students can write a thesis statement in response to the complete critical challenge.

Time for Reflection

Inherent in the writing process is reflection in preparation for and in the process of writing. Reflection on one's writing can be structured by an instructional strategy that provides for opportunities to revise. Although feedback from the instructor or peers can direct this revision, students, given adequate criteria and guidance, can engage in preliminary assessment of their own work. A series of questions provided by the instructor can prompt them to attend to aspects of significance to the critical challenge and to good writing, and encourage them to reflect on whether or not they have responded successfully to the questions.

Collegial Interaction

Although writing is typically a solitary activity, there must be opportunities for the instructor or peers to give feedback to meet the criterion of collegial interaction. The peer review process is particularly advantageous because students learn about the criteria and standards used to judge work quality, adding another dimension to their understanding through providing an additional opportunity for their engagement in CT (Tsui, 2002). Reviewer feedback can provide an opportunity for debate between author and reviewer. Rewriting for assessment can also take place. The CPR example includes a peer review process that encourages students to take a critically informed stance both with respect to other students' work and their own work. In a well-structured peer review activity, students are intensely engaged in thinking, writing, discussing, and rewriting, thus reducing instructor grading hours and providing an additional source of feedback for students. Because peer review does not always result in feedback of adequate quality, multiple peer reviews on student work are advisable. The quality of the student feedback is related to the clarity of the established criteria and the degree to which students understand these criteria.

One writing strategy definitely requiring collegial interaction is the collaborative or group writing assignment. Collaboration writing may be either *dialogical or hierarchical* (Lunsford & Ede, 1994). In dialogical collaboration, all group members work on all aspects of the project. In hierarchical collaboration, the task is divided into component parts with each group member assuming responsibility for a particular component. Dialogical collaborations are best used during exploration of an unfamiliar topic in which all students attempt to clarify terminology and acquire conceptual understanding. As a group, students may then decide collaboratively upon a common perspective or direction. Hierarchical collaboration is best used when efficiencies are sought (Lunsford & Ede, 1994) such as in the gathering, reading, and summarizing of sources. Group members may write dialogically to construct support for their thesis, but return to hierarchical writing to produce drafts of each of the sections of the supporting argument. Such collegial interaction, with group members working together through their shared writing to reach a common understanding or to propose a particular position, can be a significant condition to improving engagement in CT.

Examples of Formative Writing Activities

Examples of formative writing activities include in the moment writing, framing and reframing writing, webbing and/or concept maps, writing and rewriting a thesis statement, drafting an argument or constructing support, counterpoint writing, summaries, designing assessment questions, triple entry reports, writing of dialectical journals, connecting and transferring journals, and autobiographical journals in which students can be encouraged to write about their personal experiences in relation to course activities or content. Informal and exploratory writing activities are among the more powerful instructional strategies for promoting critical thinking and engaging students in learning.

Experiencing

Experiential instructional strategies span the range of activities from extensive out-of-class practica, internships, work placements and studio work or workshops, to short course-based activities that allow for the application of knowledge to an activity or experience. We will focus on the course-based experiential activities since potential instructional strategies in teaching for CT can include various types of role play (as in our anthropology and our nursing examples), laboratory activities, workshops, field trips and other activities. The focus in any of these strategies is on making sense of concrete experiences by working to discover their meaning. We also include in this category the types of experiences in which students engage in the fine and performing arts.

In all experiential learning strategies, the crucial factor is the quality of the reflection that students bring to bear on the experience. Although often presented as a cycle, the experiential learning process is better represented as a spiral. For examples, as students experiment with the concepts in a novel context, they may experience new or modified outcomes. Their learning involves a developmental process such that later knowledge and understanding build on and emerge from earlier knowledge and understanding.

The experiential learning cycle allows for all the reflective dispositions of CT, though these are not explicit in the process. The role of the instructor in promoting CT within experiential learning is to identify and clarify this dimension in the critical challenge and to encourage students to engage appropriately in the other two dimensions of CT, using relevant intellectual habits and intellectual deliberations.

Critical Challenges for Experiencing

The main source of the critical challenge for experiencing is the experience itself. If constructed in the course (game, simulation, role-play), the experience must involve a problematic and challenging situation relevant to students or related to something that students may encounter in the future. The frame for the critical challenge makes reference both to the source materials and to the students' experience in the role-play. In the case of reflection on personal experience, the frame will address the personal experience in relation to theoretical constructs in the course. Some experiential learning strategies have as their goal the enhanced awareness of personal and social reality as well as possible contradictions in these realities.

Although experiential sources for a critical challenge are abundant, it is the frame that will determine the quality of the CT activity in response to that source.

Time for Reflection

The experiential learning cycle has a specific phase of reflection built into the process. The challenge for the instructor is to structure the reflective process so that it can adequately represent the experiences of the students and enable them to move to the abstracting or "so what?" stage. The reflection may be done in writing (e.g., journal, laboratory log book, or essay), through conversation (e.g., small group dialogue, panel, or fishbowl), or may be reflected in subsequent actions or judgements made by the student. If the experience is recorded (as in the nursing example) the recordings can provide the opportunity for the students to reflect on their actions. Gibbs (1988) suggests that the reflection activity be a structured one so that students are encouraged to 'dig deeper' and refrain from coming to a premature closure on the experience. If this reflection activity, or debriefing, is to promote critical thinking, students should move beyond the mere description of feelings or responses to the experience. He also contends that if students do not fully engage in the interpretations of the experience, this will hinder their progression to evaluating the experience and any further action.

The following is a structured debriefing process described by Gibbs (1988) that can promote CT.

Step 1.   Prepare a comprehensive description of the experience.

Step 2.   Prepare a comprehensive description of the response (reactions/thoughts/feelings) to the experience without any analysis of this response.

Step 3.   Identify what were the positive and negative outcomes of the experience.

Step 4.   Analyze the positives and negatives of the experience.

Step 5.   Prepare general conclusions to summarize the experience in the light of this analysis.

Step 6.   Prepare specific conclusions related to personal actions, knowledge and skills, or values.

Step 7.   Develop an action plan for future similar experiences.

Collegial Interaction

Experiential learning activities allow for multiple opportunities for interaction between student and instructor, peers, or those individuals encountered in the experiential activity. Preparation for the activity will likely involve student-instructor interaction whereas within the experience there may be multiple opportunities for peer interaction.

Although there is still a need for prescriptive feedback, it is very important that students have the opportunity to debrief their experience, describing it and the congruence between what they know and what actions they took or the resultant shift in understanding. Debriefing can occur with any of the three sources identified previously. In some cases, peer debriefing may be less intimidating than debriefing with instructors or participants in the experiential setting and allow for a more honest discussion of the experience.

Experiencing Instructional Formats

Examples of experiencing instructional formats include simulations (Gibbs, 1988), role play, laboratories, games, and various field experiences.

Comprehensive Course Formats for Critical Thinking

Comprehensive course formats for CT may include any or all of the following: inquiry, problem based learning (PBL), project based learning, case based learning, and work based learning. In each of these comprehensive curriculum formats, the features of a significant critical challenge, time to reflect, and collegial interactions are prominent and provide excellent examples of 'working the content' of a course to solve problems, address provocative issues and to make meaningful evaluative judgements. All of these features contribute to the development of CT.

Assessing and Evaluating Critical Thinking

The assessment of students is a serious and often tragic enterprise.

Paul Ramsden, 1992. p. 181

Assessment, as used here, refers to the application of some 'instrument' or procedure that ends in a written, oral, or visual production by the student. Subsequently, the instructor must make a judgement about the quality of the student's production based on the criteria established for judging that production in terms of a grading system. Making such a comparative judgement and assigning an appropriate grade is the act of evaluating.

Establishing Standards for Evaluation

Once criteria for CT, the desired elements and qualities that are evidence of success, have been established, the instructor must determine how well students are demonstrating those criteria in their activities. The various levels or degrees of meeting the criteria are referred to as standards. Typically instructors are interested in the degrees of success that students demonstrate in meeting the criteria rather than whether students meet or do not meet the criteria. Therefore, the instructor needs to establish a number of standards to reflect students' varying degrees of success in meeting a criterion. Lipman (1988) describes two senses of standards:

1. Informal comparison measures (e.g., student participation in the Thursday seminar was better than in the Monday seminar).

2. Formal comparison measures with instruments and standardized units established by accepted authorities
   a. An ideal comparison (perfect or error-free performance);
   b. A minimalist comparison measure (the minimum grade average required for university admission);
   c. A normative standard for comparison (one student's average score is compared to the class mean score);
   d. An evaluative comparison against established benchmarks (depicted levels of achievement for desired criteria).

Where a single standard is used, the student production is evaluated by comparing it to that standard, with one of two outcomes. It meets the standard or it does not (e.g., accurate or inaccurate, pass or fail, complete or incomplete). Alternatively, a range of standards may be used to reflect various levels of success in comparison to the standard (e.g., unsatisfactory to outstanding; superficial to comprehensive; or 1 to 100) (Ford, 1998).

Establishing the number of levels of success depends on how finely the instructor wishes to discriminate. The usual choice is three to five levels of success but more or fewer may be warranted. The following examples, modified from Stevens and Levi (2005), illustrate descriptions of various levels of success:

1. Mastery, progressing, emerging
2. Accomplished, above average, average, developing, beginning
3. Sophisticated, competent, partially competent, no competency
4. Advanced, high intermediate, intermediate, advanced novice, novice
5. Exemplary, proficient, intermediate, novice
6. Competent, developing, beginning
7. Outstanding, competent, needs work
8. Outstanding, proficient, average, developing, emerging
9. Pass, fail
10. Letter grade
11. Level of attainment expressed as percentage.

Using Rubrics to Evaluate Critical Thinking

In keeping with the need for instructors to be explicit in their intentions and expectations of student, we recommend using descriptive benchmarks or rubrics to guide student evaluation. Such an approach will guide students in their responses. It is our judgement, and one increasingly shared by instructors (Bean, 1996), that the process of assessing and evaluating must be integrally related to students' learning. Use of rubrics in our assessment plan will facilitate student learning.

Rubrics are descriptors of various levels or standards for the work that students produce. Rubrics are the operational extension of the criteria that the instructor sets as an indicator of successful student work. As comprehensive descriptors of levels of attainment, rubrics are very useful in giving students detailed feedback, in encouraging students to use feedback to improve their future performance, and in supporting collegial interaction. As explicit statements about instructor expectations, rubrics ensure that all students are working and learning with the same information. In this way instructors are not privileging any one person or group in courses because of previous differential educational or cultural experiences (Stevens & Levi, 2005).

It is useful to clarify three terms we are using. The *criteria* for CT that the instructor sets as part of being explicit about the dimension of CT describe the best result that the student can produce. The *standards* chosen are the various levels of attainment of those criteria. The description of the level of the standard is called a *rubric*.

The resulting rubrics represent "criterion-referenced" evaluation and may be shared with students or even developed with them. As students come to understand CT and what features instructors expect, they are more likely to succeed. Since more students will be able to succeed in meeting expectations, it is likely that the traditional normal curve form of evaluation will be challenged.

In Tables 16, 17 and 18, we provide statements of rubrics for three levels of attainment – *beginning, developing, and competent* – for each of the three dimensions of CT.

Table 16
Rubrics for the Features of Intellectual Habits

Intellectual Habits	Competent Level	Developing Level	Beginning Level
Intellectual curiosity	Consistently pursues own curiosity & opportunities for CT, going beyond readily available information	Inconsistent in pursuing opportunities for CT in going beyond readily available information	Seldom, if ever, pursues opportunities for CT in going beyond readily available information
Respect for truth and reason	Consistently seeks most sustainable judgement	Inconsistently or partially seeks most sustainable judgement or may do so in limited, self-serving way	Seldom, if ever, seeks most sustainable judgement
Fair and open-mindedness	Consistently seeks out alternative position(s) & strives to understand them as if one's own, realistic in weighing relative merit, and open to change if the evidence warrants	Inconsistently or partially seeks out alternative position(s) to try to understand them, realistic in weighing relative merit, and/or open to change if evidence warrants	Seldom, if ever, seeks out alternative position(s) to try to understand them; not open to change
Tolerance for ambiguity and complexity	Consistently patient with and explicit about limitations of one's current level of understanding	Inconsistently patient with and explicit about limitations of one's current level of understanding	Seldom, if ever, is patient with and explicit about limitations of one's current level of understanding
Intellectual courage to take a position	Consistently takes a position, even if unpopular, if one thinks it is more defensible than other positions or the morally right thing to do	Inconsistently takes a position, even if unpopular, if one thinks it is more defensible than other positions or the morally right thing to do	Seldom, if ever, takes an unpopular position, even if one thinks it is more defensible than other positions or the morally right thing to do
Intellectual work ethic	Consistently perseveres to do best, even when faces unexpected challenges	Inconsistently perseveres to do best when faced with unexpected challenges	Seldom, if ever, perseveres to do best when faced with unexpected challenges
Willingness to engage in collaborative inquiry	Consistently respectful of different levels of knowledge and seeks out and contributes to responsible constructive interactions	Inconsistently respectful of different levels of knowledge and/or seeks out and contributes to responsible constructive interactions	Seldom, if ever, respectful of different levels of knowledge or responsible toward constructive interactions

Table 17
Rubrics for the Processes of Intellectual Deliberations

Intellectual Deliberations	Competent Level	Developing Level	Beginning Level
Identifying the challenge situation or task for inquiry that will lead to CT judgements	Consistently provides plausible identification of challenge situation or task in need of critical judgements	Inconsistently provides plausible identification of challenge situation or task in need of critical judgements	Seldom, if ever, provides plausible identification of challenge situation or task in need of critical judgements
Gathering, interpreting, and understanding background information and other evidence relevant to the critical challenge	Consistently selects/uses information that is relevant and sufficient for the context of the challenge situation or task to progress toward sustainable judgement Consistently provides accurate or plausible interpretation of background information and other evidence relevant to the challenge	Inconsistently selects/uses information that is relevant and sufficient for the context of the challenge situation or task to progress toward sustainable judgement Inconsistently provides accurate or plausible interpretation of background information and other evidence relevant to the challenge	Seldom, if ever, selects/uses information that is relevant and sufficient for the context of the challenge situation or task to progress toward sustainable judgement Seldom, if ever, provides accurate or plausible interpretation of background information and other evidence relevant to the challenge
Selecting and applying thinking strategies that are relevant to the type of inquiry and informed by the background information	Consistent selection of relevant inquiry thinking strategies that effectively contribute to a sustainable judgement Consistent appropriate application of inquiry thinking strategies	Inconsistent selection of relevant inquiry thinking strategies that effectively contribute to a sustainable judgement Inconsistent appropriate application of inquiry thinking strategies	Seldom, if ever, selects relevant inquiry thinking strategies that effectively contribute to a sustainable judgement Seldom, if ever, appropriate application of inquiry thinking strategies
Making judgements based on criteria relevant to the kind of judgement required	Consistent selection of criteria congruent with the kind of judgement and mode of inquiry Consistent application of criteria congruent with kind of judgement and mode of inquiry	Inconsistent selection of criteria congruent with the kind of judgement and mode of inquiry Inconsistent application of criteria congruent with kind of judgement and mode of inquiry	Seldom, if ever, selects criteria congruent with the kind of judgement and mode of inquiry Seldom, if ever, applies criteria congruent with kind of judgement and mode of inquiry
Constructing justification for judgements based on the adequacy of the intellectual dimensions applied in thinking through the critical challenge and the congruence between support and conclusions	Consistent plausible justification that explicitly evaluates the quality of support for conclusion and the strength of congruence between support and concluding judgement Consistently provides plausible account of why concluding judgement is more sustainable than other options at this time	Inconsistent or partial plausible justification that explicitly evaluates the quality of support for conclusion and the strength of congruence between support and concluding judgement Inconsistently or partially provides plausible account of why concluding judgement is more sustainable than other options at this time	Seldom, if ever, provides plausible justification that explicitly evaluates the quality of support for conclusion and the strength of congruence between support and concluding judgement Seldom, if ever, provides plausible account of why concluding judgement is more sustainable than other options at this time

Table 18
Rubrics for the Features of a Reflexive Disposition

Reflexive Disposition	Competent Level	Developing Level	Beginning Level
Plan ahead for integration of intellectual habits, intellectual deliberations and reflexive dispositions to maximize the quality of one's thinking	Where appropriate, consistently engages in planning ahead to maximize the quality of thinking; planning consistently reflects striving toward relevant and sufficient integration of intellectual habits, intellectual deliberations, and reflexive dispositions	Inconsistently engages in planning ahead to maximize the quality of thinking; planning, when done, inconsistently reflects striving for relevant and sufficient integration of dimensions of critical thinking	Seldom, if ever, engages in planning ahead to maximize the quality of thinking; planning, if done, unlikely reflects striving for integration of dimensions of critical thinking
Monitor the use of intellectual habits, intellectual deliberations, and reflexive dispositions during their application to improve the quality of one's thinking	Where appropriate, consistently engages in monitoring the quality of thinking while thinking to improve the quality of one's thinking; monitoring reveals consistent striving for more plausible, coherent, and sufficient evaluations and justifications for/against adjustments in the use of intellectual habits, intellectual deliberations, and reflexive disposition	Inconsistently engages in monitoring thinking while thinking to improve the quality of one's thinking; monitoring, when done, is inconsistent in striving for more plausible, coherent, and/or sufficient evaluations and justifications for/against adjustments in the use of dimensions of critical thinking	Seldom, if ever, engages in monitoring thinking while thinking to improve the quality of one's thinking; monitoring, if done, unlikely strives for plausible, coherent, or sufficient evaluations and justifications for/against adjustments in the use of dimensions of critical thinking
Reflect back on the quality of integration of intellectual habits, intellectual deliberations, and reflexive disposition in order to improve one's future thinking	Where appropriate, consistently reflects back on thinking to improve future thinking; reflections on thinking consistently strive toward more plausible, coherent and sufficient evaluations & justifications for/against adjustments to the use of intellectual habits, intellectual deliberations, and reflexive dispositions	Inconsistently reflects back on thinking to improve one's future thinking; reflections, when done, inconsistently exhibits plausible, coherent or sufficient evaluations and justifications for/against adjustments to the integration of dimensions of critical thinking	Seldom, if ever, engages in reflecting back on thinking to improve one's future thinking; reflections, if done, unlikely to exhibit evaluations or justifications for/against adjustments to the integration of dimensions of critical thinking

Rubrics for evaluating student engagement in CT, like definitions, dimensions, and criteria, should be determined before the instructor begins teaching the course. While making such rubrics explicit is a time consuming activity, the instructor will need to do this comprehensively only once. When criteria and rubrics for CT are established, they will only require review and modification so as to apply rubrics to specific assignments and examinations. Rubrics not only increase the quality of the feedback that instructors can provide students but also improve the quality of student production and decrease instructor marking time.

Each of the four instructional activities we have used as examples is congruent to varying degrees with our model of CT. We represent some of the more salient aspects of the three CT dimensions in several rubrics to be found in the Appendices. Such representation gives guidance to instructors about how to write rubrics for the dimensions they have identified for CT.

Methods of Assessment

Regardless of the form of assessment chosen by instructors, a critical challenge must be central to the process. Instructors are able to assess the quality of students' engagement in CT only if they provide opportunities for students to demonstrate their proficiency. The types of opportunities instructors provide for students to learn CT should influence the nature of the assessment. In a course structured on a PBL model, assessment must address complex problems that necessitate integrating the dimensions of CT. Students must be asked to demonstrate the processes and understanding for which they have been prepared through instruction and engagement in CT.

Due to the nature of CT, the tool or instrument that instructors use for assessment must have the following three characteristics:

1. It presents a critical challenge situation or trigger.
2. It requires an evaluative judgement.
3. It requires justification for that judgement.

Unless students are provided the opportunity to justify their judgements, comprehensive assessment of their engagement in and mastery of CT is compromised.

These requirements for assessment result in a student-produced outcome that can easily and appropriately be evaluated. Assessment methods should be aligned or congruent with both learning outcomes and choices of instructional strategies. With guidance on the dimensions of CT and clarity on the established criteria and standards, students can progress steadily and be able to demonstrate outcomes that reflect their successful engagement in CT.

Course Climate and Conditions for Supporting Critical Thinking

Instructors must create an intellectual and emotional climate that encourages students' taking risks.

Bonwell and Eisen, 1991, p. 22

In all the instructional strategies that we have reviewed, students are encouraged to take ownership of their learning through tackling critical challenges. Students must learn to question their own thoughts and ideas as well as those of their peers and appropriate authorities. We also provide appropriate opportunities for students to be intellectually active and engaged in class and to work at learning with as much effort as instructors are giving to their teaching. The evidence is compelling that in this learning environment student engagement in CT will flourish. Unfortunately, experiencing such a learning environment is so uncommon that some students may be discouraged by the level of effort and discomfort involved.

Because engagement in CT is central to post-secondary education, it is worth the effort to address students' preference for the more familiar and traditional instructor-directed lecture approach as well as to overcome their resistance to views of knowledge that involve making evaluative judgement. We began with a model (Figure 1) that suggests course climate and conditions form the context and foundation for the success of teaching for CT. This perspective on teaching and learning is well supported in the literature.

A number of common themes related to climate and condition in teaching for CT cluster about the concept of building a *community of learners.* The implication of working to create a sense of community in a course is that students feel a part of this community and know that others in the community, including the instructor, will contribute to the common goal of learning.

Instructors must be respectful of students and their ideas if they expect them rise to the challenge of engagement in CT. Instructors who respect students are sensitive to their differences and respond thoughtfully to both verbal and nonverbal behaviours (Brookfield, 1987). They seek conversation with students and build on students' ideas, making clear connections among course content, the broader society, and students' prior knowledge. Teachers also signal their respect for student learning in the quality and quantity of feedback they provide. Feedback to students is most effective when it is explicit, reinforcing what students are doing well and providing guidance in areas of weakness. In describing the hospitable teacher, Meyers (1986) states, "The teacher has to take away the veil covering many students' intellectual lives, and help them see that their own life experiences, their own insights and convictions, their own intuitions and formulations are worth serious attention" (p.68).

Instructors can serve as powerful role models for engagement in CT. Instructors should be willing to discuss areas about which they have questions and that remain ambiguous and unclear. Having a discussion that generates more questions than answers demonstrates to students the patience needed for intellectual development. The generation of questions often sparks students' interest, arouses curiosity, and encourages students to express their personal perspectives and raise issues about which they are uncertain.

As part of creating course conditions for CT, instructors should be explicit and transparent about what they mean by the term CT and its dimensions. This detail and clarity contribute significantly to students' learning. Using a common language helps students to grasp the complexities of CT and to learn course content.

Students appear to be more responsive to less traditional methods of instruction if they have a clear sense of the intention of the methods and the connections to the course outcomes. Instructors who have developed informative learning outcomes for their courses can share their aspirations and goals with students and discuss the reasons informing their instructional approaches. Clearly stated and comprehensive learning outcomes also provide instructors with opportunities to make explicit the various approaches to assessment and how these are integral to student learning.

Instructors who encourage engagement in CT as integral to their active learning courses should make this orientation evident to students from the first class. A discussion of course and learning expectations, reinforced by questions that encourage students to think about the relevance of the area of study that they are about to begin, is a simple but effective foundation for that first CT interaction with students.

To summarize this final section on teaching for CT, course climate and conditions should be primary considerations. Particular actions that instructors can take to model CT and to provide support to students in engaging in CT include the following:

- Being explicit about CT, its dimensions and criteria for success

- Discussing ground rules for respectful collegial interaction

- Inviting student conversation and interaction from the very first class

- Engaging in CT activities consistently throughout the course

- Providing timely and supportive feedback to encourage CT

- Modelling respectful interaction with students individually and with the class as a whole as integral to the practice of CT

- Being explicit about instructor aspirations for students' learning and discussing and inviting student feedback on intended learning outcomes.

Teaching for CT is challenging and requires considerable time and effort. However, when students shift from taken-for-granted perspectives based on subjective and superficial knowledge to more thoughtful, deeper, and reasoned understanding, the benefit is undeniable.

Appendix 1
Chemistry: Calibrated Peer Review (CPR)

1. Intellectual Habits

Intellectual curiosity		
Competent	Developing	Beginning
Consistently goes beyond materials provided	Inconsistent in going beyond materials provided	Seldom, if ever, goes beyond materials provided

Intellectual work ethic		
Competent	Developing	Beginning
Essays consistently exhibit evidence of perseverance to ensure congruence with all expected criteria, and beyond if feasible, at the highest level of competency	Essays inconsistently reflect perseverance to ensure congruence with expected criteria	Essays seldom, if ever, exhibit evidence of perseverance to ensure congruence with expected criteria
Evaluations of peer essays consistently show evidence of perseverance to provide relevant, plausible, and comprehensive responses that are strong in congruence with the actual quality of essays	Evaluations of peer essays are mixed in evidence of perseverance	Evaluations of peer essays seldom, if ever, exhibit perseverance

2. Intellectual Deliberations

Gather, interpret and represent information relevant to the challenge		
Competent	Developing	Beginning
Consistent in making accurate or plausible and comprehensive interpretations	Inconsistent in making accurate or plausible and comprehensive interpretations	Seldom, if ever, provides accurate or plausible and comprehensive interpretations

Make judgements based on criteria relevant to the kind of judgement required		
Competent	Developing	Beginning
Consistently makes plausible judgements about the congruence between the essays and criteria provided, and support in justifications for their judgements is relevant and sufficient to make a strong case	Inconsistently makes plausible judgements about the congruence between essays and criteria provided and support in justifications for their judgements, if offered, may be mixed in relevance and sufficiency to make a strong case	Seldom if ever, makes plausible judgements about the congruence between essays and criteria provided and their support, if offered, is neither relevant or sufficient to make even a weak case

3. Reflexive Disposition

Reflect back on the quality of intellectual deliberations to improve them		
Competent	Developing	Beginning
Consistent engagement in reflections; reflections consistently lead to plausible evaluations and justifications with potential to improve accuracy/plausibility and comprehensiveness of interpretations and congruence among essay, evaluations of essays, and the criteria provided to students	Inconsistent engagement in reflections that lead to plausible evaluations and justifications and/or reflections do not consistently lead to potential to improve quality of interpretations and the congruency among essay, evaluations of essays, and the criteria provided to them	Lack of evidence of engagement in reflections or reflections seldom, if ever, lead to plausible evaluations and justifications

Appendix 2
Anthropology: Role-Play

1. Intellectual Habits

Fair-mindedness		
Competent	Developing	Beginning
Deliberations consistently consider in a balanced way the needs of both tribes. Conclusions consistently reflect outcomes that would plausibly be acceptable (e.g., safe, fair, and feasible) to both groups.	Deliberations inconsistently consider in a balanced way the needs of both tribes. Conclusions are inconsistent in reflecting outcomes that would plausibly be acceptable to both groups.	Deliberations seldom, if ever, consider in a balanced way the needs of both tribes. Conclusions seldom, if ever, reflect outcomes that would plausibly be acceptable to both groups.

Willingness to engage in collaborative inquiry		
Competent	Developing	Beginning
Consistently display respectful interactions with members of both tribal groups Consistently seek and engage in opportunities to collaborate with members of their own tribe as they inquire into the range of relevant perspectives in order to find ways to resolve the conflict that are acceptable to all who will be impacted by the outcome of the decision	Inconsistently display respectful interactions with members of both tribal groups Inconsistently seek or agree to opportunities to collaborate with members of their own tribe in order to find ways to resolve the conflict	Seldom, if ever, display respectful interactions with members of either tribal group Seldom, if ever, seek or agree to opportunities to collaborate with members of their own tribe in order to find ways to resolve the conflict

2. Intellectual Deliberations

Interpret and represent background information relevant to the critical challenge		
Competent	Developing	Beginning
Consistently engage in making accurate or plausible and comprehensive interpretations of the information provided by the instructor Consistently make relevant and comprehensive connections among ideas about competing needs for land use, the nature of past interactions between tribal groups, and protocols valued by each group toward informed evaluations of the relative merit of alternative negotiation strategies toward an effective resolution of the conflict	Inconsistently engage in making accurate or plausible and comprehensive interpretations of the information Inconsistently engage in making relevant and comprehensive connections among ideas, protocols, and alternative negotiation strategies toward informed evaluations of the relative merit of alternative negotiation strategies	Seldom, if ever, engage in making accurate or plausible and comprehensive interpretations of the information Seldom, if ever, engage in making relevant and comprehensive connections among ideas, protocols, and alternative negotiation strategies toward informed evaluations of the relative merit of alternative negotiation strategies

Make judgements based on criteria relevant to the kind of judgement required

Competent	Developing	Beginning
Consistently engage in identifying criteria that are relevant and sufficient to the judgement being made—in this case the alternative negotiation strategies that are plausibly most likely to be acceptable to both groups because they are most safe, fair, and feasible when viewed from relevant perspectives Consistently and systematically apply relevant and sufficient criteria to make plausible evaluations and judgements about the relative safety and fairness of the range of alternative negotiation strategies as they pertain to those affected, as well as for the relative feasibility of alternatives in light of the adequacy of time and resources available	Inconsistently engage in identifying criteria that are relevant and sufficient to the judgement being made or may identify relevant criteria but apply them inconsistently to alternatives as they pertain to relevant points of view Inconsistent in systematic and fair application of relevant and/or sufficient criteria to judgements among alternative negotiation strategies as they pertain to relevant points of view	Seldom, if ever, engage in identifying criteria that are relevant to the judgement being made Seldom, if ever, systematically or fairly apply relevant and sufficient criteria to judgements among alternative negotiation strategies as they pertain to relevant points of view

3. Reflexive Disposition

Reflect back on the quality of intellectual habits and intellectual deliberations

Competent	Developing	Beginning
Consistently, as appropriate, engage in reflections that consistently make explicit, plausible, and comprehensive connections among the quality of intellectual deliberations, consistency in being fair and open-minded, and the effectiveness of negotiations and judgements toward conflict resolution Consistently engage in reflections, as appropriate, that consistently identify or consider the importance of relevant background information to generating a range of viable alternative negotiation strategies and to understanding the implications that each alternative could have for meeting the conflicting needs of each tribe Consistently engage in reflections, as appropriate, that consistently identify/consider a plausible range of benefits of respecting relevant protocols to effective negotiations and conflict resolution	Inconsistently engage in reflections and if so engaged, inconsistently make explicit, plausible, and comprehensive connections among intellectual habits, intellectual deliberations, and the effectiveness of negotiations and judgements toward conflict resolution Inconsistently engage in reflections that identify/consider the importance of relevant background information to generating a range of viable alternatives and to understanding the implications that each alternative could have for meeting the conflicting needs of each tribe Inconsistently engage in reflections that identify/consider a plausible range of benefits of respecting relevant tribal protocols to effective negotiations and conflict resolution	Seldom, if ever, engage in reflections that make explicit, plausible, and comprehensive connections among the quality of intellectual habits, intellectual deliberations and the effectiveness of negotiations and judgements toward conflict resolution Seldom, if ever, engage in reflections that identify/consider the importance of relevant background information to generating a range of viable alternatives and to understanding the implications that each alternative could have for meeting the conflicting needs of each tribe Seldom, if ever, engage in reflections that identify/consider a plausible range of benefits of respecting relevant protocols to effective negotiations and conflict resolution

Appendix 3
Art History: Reflective Reading

1. Intellectual Habits

Intellectual curiosity		
Competent	Developing	Beginning
The ideas and questions relevant to the art history text that were selected, shared, and justified consistently reflect a curiosity about ideas that could plausibly matter to someone Consistently engage in going beyond assigned reading to inquire further into personally important or interesting ideas and questions	The ideas or questions that were selected, shared, and justified inconsistently reflect a curiosity about ideas that could plausibly matter to someone Inconsistently engage in going beyond assignment reading to inquire further into relevant ideas or questions	Seldom, if ever, select, share, and justify ideas or questions relevant to the art history text that reflect an intellectual curiosity about ideas that could plausibly matter to someone Seldom, if ever, go beyond assigned readings to inquire further into relevant ideas or questions to inquire into ideas

2. Intellectual Deliberations

Interpret information and understand information relevant to challenge		
Competent	Developing	Beginning
Consistently engage in selecting burning ideas and questions that are consistent in relevance to ideas in the art history text Consistently strive for deeper understanding by seeking further clarification, elaboration, support, extension, or by challenging the adequacy of the ideas in the art history text	Inconsistently select ideas and questions that are relevant to ideas in the art history text which may reflect either inadequate understanding and/or interest	Seldom, if ever, selects ideas and questions that have any relevance to ideas in the art text which may reflect either inadequate understanding and/or interest

Make judgements based on criteria relevant to the challenge		
Competent	Developing	Beginning
Ideas and questions selected consistently align with criteria that describe what significant and burning ideas/issues look like--ideas for which the outcome of what one believes or does would matter greatly to someone It is consistently plausible that ideas/questions selected are of personal interest to student	Ideas and questions inconsistently align with criteria that describe what significant and burning ideas/issues look like It is inconsistently plausible that ideas/questions could be of personal interest to student	Ideas and questions seldom, if ever, align with criteria that describe what significant and burning ideas/issues look like It is unlikely plausible that ideas/questions could be of personal interest to student

Identify a task for an inquiry		
Competent	Developing	Beginning
Consistently identify ideas for inquiry that logically follow from the ideas in the text but which are not answered in the text	Inconsistently identify ideas for inquiry that are relevant to ideas in the text and which are not answered in the text	Seldom, if ever, identify ideas for inquiry that are relevant to ideas in the text, or if they do, the answers to questions may be found in the text

Appendix 4
Nursing: Audiotaped Interaction

1. Intellectual Habits

Intellectual work ethic

Competent	Developing	Beginning
Consistent evidence of perseverance toward systematic, plausible and comprehensive interpretations & representations of client-nurse interactions	Inconsistent evidence of perseverance toward systematic, plausible and comprehensive interpretations & representations of client-nurse interactions	Seldom, if ever, exhibits evidence of perseverance toward systematic, plausible and comprehensive interpretations of client-nurse interactions
Consistently persevere toward evaluations congruent with what relevant parties would agree is the actual quality of client-nurse interactions	Inconsistent evidence of perseverance toward evaluations congruent with what relevant parties would agree is the actual quality of client-nurse interactions	Seldom, if ever, exhibits evidence of perseverance toward evaluations that are congruent with what relevant parties would agree is the actual quality of client-nurse interactions

Open-mindedness

Competent	Developing	Beginning
Consistently exhibit openness to alternative interpretations about the quality of client-nurse interactions	Inconsistent evidence of being open to alternative interpretations	Seldom, if ever, exhibits evidence of being open to alternative interpretations
Consistently exhibit openness to using alternative interpretations about the quality of client-nurse interactions if there is a compelling reason to do so (e.g., potential to improve the quality of client-nurse interactions)	Inconsistent evidence of being open to using alternative interpretations about the quality of client-nurse interactions to try to improve the quality of client-nurse interactions	

2. Intellectual Deliberations

Interpret and represent information relevant to challenge

Competent	Developing	Beginning
Consistently provide relevant, plausible, and comprehensive interpretations of the nature of the challenge, the intent of guiding questions, and the samples to guide interpretations and analyses	Inconsistently provide relevant, plausible, and/or comprehensive interpretations	Seldom, if ever, represent relevant, plausible, and/or comprehensive interpretations
Consistently represent relevant, plausible, and comprehensive interpretations of the nature of client-nurse interactions	Inconsistently represent relevant, plausible, and comprehensive interpretations	Seldom, if ever, represent relevant, plausible, comprehensive interpretations

Make judgements based on criteria relevant to kind of judgement

Competent	Developing	Beginning
Judgements are consistently congruent with the quality of relational capacity in client-nurse interactions	Judgements are inconsistent in congruence with the quality of relational capacity in client-nurse interactions	Judgements are seldom, if ever, congruent with the quality of relational capacity in client-nurse interactions
Judgements are consistently congruent with potential to effectively maximize relational capacity	Judgements are inconsistent in congruence with potential to effectively maximize relational capacity	Judgements are seldom, if ever, congruent with potential to effectively maximize relational capacity

Construct justification for judgements

Competent	Developing	Beginning
Justifications consistently provide relevant, plausible, and sufficient reasons/evidence to make a compelling case for the congruence among intellectual habits, intellectual deliberations, and judgements about the level of relational capacity as it evolved throughout the course	Justifications are inconsistent in providing relevant, plausible, and sufficient support for congruence among intellectual habits, intellectual deliberations, and judgements	Justifications seldom, if ever, provide relevant, plausible, and sufficient support for congruence among intellectual habits, intellectual deliberations, and judgements
Justifications consistently select and represent plausible, relevant, and sufficient evidence from audio-tapes and from experiences to provide sustainable support for judgements about relational capacity	Justifications are inconsistent in selecting and representing plausible, relevant and sufficient evidence from audio-tapes and from experiences to provide sustainable support for judgements	Justifications seldom, if ever, select and represent plausible, relevant and sufficient evidence from audio-tapes and from experiences to support for judgements

3. Reflexive disposition

Planning to improve thinking

Competent	Developing	Beginning
Consistently questions the adequacy of thinking to achieve both stronger selection and stronger application of relevant and sufficient habits, deliberations, and reflexive disposition	Inconsistently questions the adequacy of thinking to achieve both stronger selection and stronger application of relevant and sufficient habits, deliberations, and reflexive disposition	Seldom, if ever, questions the adequacy of thinking to achieve both stronger selection and stronger application of relevant and sufficient habits, deliberations, and reflexive disposition
Consistent in using evaluative reflections about relational capacity to help plan ahead to improve the overall quality of selection and application of deliberations, habits, and reflexive disposition in order to maximize relational capacity for future interactions	Inconsistent in using evaluative reflections about relational capacity to help plan ahead to improve the overall quality of deliberations, habits, and reflexive disposition	Seldom, if ever, use evaluative reflections about relational capacity to help plan ahead to improve the overall quality of deliberations, habits, and reflexive disposition

Monitor thinking in action

Competent	Developing	Beginning
Reflections consistently provide a relevant, plausible, and sufficient account of feelings during client-nurse interactions	Reflections are inconsistent in providing a relevant, plausible, and/or sufficient account of feelings during client-nurse interactions	Reflections seldom, if ever, provide relevant, plausible, or sufficient account of feelings during client-nurse interactions
Reflections are consistently congruent with the nature of the client-nurse interactions	Reflections are inconsistent in congruence with the nature of client-nurse interactions	Reflections seldom, if ever, are congruent with the nature of client-nurse interactions

Reflect back on thinking to improve thinking

Competent	Developing	Beginning
Reflections on interactions consistently reveal evidence of striving toward plausible and comprehensive judgements about congruence among espoused values, beliefs, and actions and those values, beliefs and actions that are evident in responses	Inconsistent successful engagement in reflections on interactions toward relevant, plausible, and comprehensive judgments about congruence among espoused values, beliefs, and actions and those values, beliefs and actions that are evident in responses	Seldom, if ever, engage in reflections on interactions that reveal evidence of striving toward plausible and comprehensive judgements about congruence among their espoused values, beliefs, and actions and those values, beliefs and actions that are evident in their responses
Reflections consistently re-align actions to fit beliefs toward plausibly more effective relational capacity or adjust beliefs to fit actions that plausibly have more potential to maximize relational capacity	Inconsistent successful engagement in reflection to re-align beliefs and actions, toward plausibly improved relational capacity	Seldom, if ever, engage successfully in reflections that lead to re-aligning beliefs and actions toward plausibly improved relational capacity

References

Baron, J. B., & Sternberg, R. J. (1987). *Teaching thinking skills: Theory and practice.* New York: Freeman.

Bean, J. C. (1996). *Engaging ideas: The professor's guide to integrating writing, critical thinking, and active learning in the classroom.* San Francisco, CA: Jossey-Bass.

Biggs, J. B. (1987). *Student approaches to learning and studying.* Melbourne: Australian Council for Educational Research.

Biggs, J. B. (1993). What do inventories of students' learning process really measure? A theoretical review and clarification. *British Journal of Educational Psychology, 83,* 3-9.

Bohne, C., Brunk, C., & Kambourelli, S. (Speakers). (2002). What is critical thinking? [Video Recording]. (Available from the Learning and Teaching Centre, University of Victoria, British Columbia, Canada).

Boisvert, J. (1996). Formation de la pensée critique au collegial. Étude de cas sur développement de la pensée critique en premiere année du collegial dans un cours de psychologie. *Cegep Saint-Jean-sur-Richelieu,* 198.

Bonwell, C. C., & Eison, J. A. (1991). *Active learning: Creating excitement in the classroom* (Vol. 2). Washington, DC: School of Education and Human Development, George Washington University.

Boxler, H. M. (2002). *Quest for the Grail? Searching for critical thinking in adult education.* Paper presented at the 40th Annual Adult Education Research Conference. Raleigh, NC.

Bransford, J., Brown, A., & Cocking, R. (Eds.). (2000). *How people learn: Brain, mind, experience, and school.* Washington, DC: National Academy Press.

Brookfield, S. D. (1983). *Adult learning, adult education and the community.* Milton Keynes, UK: Open University Press.

Brookfield, S. (1987). *Developing critical thinkers: Challenging adults to explore alternative ways of thinking and acting.* Milton Keynes, UK: Open University Press.

Brookfield, S. (1995). *Becoming a critically reflective teacher* (1st ed.). San Francisco: Jossey-Bass.

Browne, M. N., & Keeley, S. M. (1998). *Asking the right questions: A guide to critical thinking* (5th ed.). Upper Saddle River, N.J.: Prentice Hall.

Bruffee, K. A. (1999). *Collaborative learning: Higher education, interdependence, and the authority of knowledge* (2nd ed.). Baltimore, Md.: John Hopkins University Press.

Bruner, J. S. (1966). *Toward a theory of instruction.* Cambridge, MA: Harvard University Press.

Carroll, L. (1969). *Alice in wonderland.* Toronto: McClelland and Stewart.

Case, R. (1997a). Beyond inert facts and concepts: Teaching for understanding. In R. Case & P. Clark (Eds.), *The Canadian anthology of social studies: Issues and strategies for teachers* (pp. 141-152). Burnaby, B.C.: Field Relations and Teacher In-service Education, Faculty of Education, Simon Fraser University.

Case, R. (1997b).   Assessment criteria and standards. In R. Case & P. Clark (Eds.), *The Canadian anthology of social studies: Issues and strategies for teachers* (pp. 402-408). Burnaby, B.C.: Field Relations and Teacher In-service Education, Faculty of Education, Simon Fraser University.

Case, R., & Wright, I. (1997). Taking seriously the teaching of critical thinking. In R. Case & P. Clark (Eds.), *The Canadian anthology of social studies: Issues and strategies for teachers* (pp. 179-193). Burnaby, B.C.: Field Relations and Teacher In-service Education, Faculty of Education, Simon Fraser University.

Chickering, A. W., & Gamson, Z. F. (1987). "Seven Principles for Good Practice in Undergraduate Education." *AAHE Bulletin*, 39(7), 3–7.

Christensen, C. R. (1982). *Teaching by the case method*. Boston, Mass.: Division of Research Harvard Business School.

Cleary, L. M., & Peacock, T. D. (1998). *Collected wisdom: American Indian education*. Boston: Allyn & Bacon.

Collison, G., Elbaum B., Haavind S., & Tinker R. (2000). *Facilitating online learning: Effective strategies for moderators*. Madison, WI: Atwood Pub.

Dewey, J. (1910). *How we think*. Boston: D.C. Heath and Co.

Donald, J. G. (2002). *Learning to think: Disciplinary perspectives* (1st ed.). San Francisco: Jossey-Bass.

Elbow, P. (1997). High stakes and low stakes in assigning and responding to writing. In M. D. Sorcinelli & P. Elbow (Eds.), *Assigning and responding to writing in the disciplines*. San Francisco: Jossey-Bass.

Endres, B. (1996). *Habermas and critical thinking*. Retrieved February 16, 2004, from http://www.ed.uiuc.edu/EPS/PES-Yearbook/96_docs/endres.html

Ennis, R. H. (1987). A taxonomy of critical thinking dispositions and abilities. In J. Baron & R. Sternberg (Eds.), *Teaching thinking skills: Theory and practice* (pp. 9–26). New York: Freeman.

Ennis, R. H. (1996). *Critical thinking*. Upper Saddle River, NJ: Prentice Hall.

Ennis, R.H., & Weir, E. (1985). *The Ennis-Weir critical thinking essay test*. Pacific Grove, CA: Midwest Publications.

Entwistle, N. J. (1981). *Styles of learning and teaching: An integrated outline of educational psychology for students, teachers and lecturers*. Chichester, New York: Wiley.

Facione, P. A. (1990). *Executive summary of critical thinking: A statement of expert consensus for purposes of educational assessment and instruction, including all tables, findings and recommendations of The Delphi Report prepared for the American Philosophical Association by Peter A. Facione (Santa Clara University)*. Millbrae, Calif.: California Academic Press.

Fink, L. D. (2003). *Creating significant learning experiences: An integrated approach to designing college courses* (1st ed.). San Francisco, Calif.: Jossey-Bass.

Fisher, K. (2003). Demystifying critical reflection: Defining criteria for assessment. *Higher Education Research and Development, 22*(3), 313-325.

Ford, C. L. (1998). *Educating preservice teachers to teach for an evaluative view of knowledge and critical thinking in elementary social studies.* Unpublished doctoral dissertation, University of Victoria, British Columbia, Canada.

Foundation for Critical Thinking (2004). *Critical thinking glossary: An educator's guide to critical thinking terms and concepts.* Retrieved January 19, 2004, from http://www.criticalthinking.org/resources/articles/glossary.shtml#JL

Fox, M. A., & Hackerman, N. (Eds.). (2003). *Evaluating and improving undergraduate teaching in science, technology, engineering, and mathematics.* Washington, D.C.: National Academies Press.

Freire, P. (1993). *Pedagogy of the oppressed* (M. B. Ramos, Trans. 2nd ed.). London: Penguin Books.

Garrison, R. (2004). *Inquiry and critical thinking.* Retrieved April 5, 2004, from http://commons.ucalgary.ca/documents/ReflectiveInquiry.pdf

Gibbs, G. (1988). *Learning by doing: A guide to teaching and learning methods.* Retrieved September 18, 2004, from http://www2.glos.ac.uk/gdn/gibbs/

Gokhale, A. A. (1995). Collaborative learning enhances critical thinking. *Journal of Technology Education, 7*(1), 22-30.

Haas, P. F., & Keeley, S. M. (1998). Coping with faculty resistance to teaching critical thinking. *College Teaching, 46*(2), 316-322.

Habermas, J. (1990). *Moral consciousness and communicative action.* Cambridge, Mass.: MIT Press.

Halpern, D. F. (1998). Teaching critical thinking for transfer across domains: Dispositions, skills, structure training and metacognitive monitoring. *American Psychologist, 53*(4), 449-455.

Hamm, C. M. (1989). *Philosophical issues in education: An introduction.* Philadelphia, PA: The Falmer Press.

Jenlink, P., & Carr, A.A. (1996). Conversation as a medium for change in education. *Educational Technology, January-February,* 31-38.

Keeley, S. M., Browne, M.N., & Kreutzer, J.S. (1982). A comparison of freshmen and seniors on general and specific essay tests of critical thinking. *Research in Higher Education, 17,* 139-154.

Keeley, S. M. (1992). Are college students learning the critical skill of finding assumptions? *College Student Journal, 26,* 316-322.

Keeley, S. M., Shemberg, K.M., Cowell B.S., & Zinnbauer, B. J. (1995). Coping with student resistance to critical thinking: What the psychotherapy literature can tell us. *College Teaching, 43*(4), 140-145.

King, P. M., Wood, P.K., & Mines, R.A. (1990). Critical thinking among college and graduate students. *Review of Higher Education, 13,* 167-185.

Kitchener, K. S., & King, P.M. (1990). The reflective judgement model: Transforming assumptions about knowing. In J. Masteri & Associates (Ed.), *Fostering critical reflection in adulthood.* San Francisco: Jossey-Bass.

Kurfiss, J. G. (1988). Critical thinking theory, research, practice, and possibilities [microform]. Washington, D.C.: Association for the Study of Higher Education.

Langsdorf, L. (1988). Ethical and logical analysis as human sciences. *Human Studies, 11*, 43-64.

Lather, P. (1989). Ideology and methodological attitude. *Journal of Curriculum Theorizing, 9*(2), 7-26.

Lipman, M. (1988). *Critical thinking: What can it be?* Upper Montclair, N.J.: Institute for Critical Thinking Montclair State College.

Lipman, M. (1991). *Thinking in education.* Cambridge, New York: Cambridge University Press.

Lunsford, A., & Ede, L. (1994). Collaborative authorship and the teaching of writing. In M. Woodmansee & P. Jaszi (Eds.), *The construction of authorship: Textual appropriation in law and literature* (pp. 417-438). Durham: Duke University Press.

Maki, P. (2004). *Assessing for learning: Building a sustainable commitment across the institution.* Sterling, VA: Stylus Publishing.

Mazur, E. (1997). *Peer instruction: A user's manual.* Upper Saddle River, N.J.: Prentice Hall.

McPeck, J. E. (1990). *Teaching critical thinking: Dialogue and dialectic.* New York: Routledge.

Meyers, C. (1986). *Teaching students to think critically* (1st ed.). San Francisco: Jossey-Bass.

Norris, S. P. (1992). *The generalizability of critical thinking: Multiple perspectives on an educational ideal.* New York: Teachers College Press.

Pascarella, E. T. (1989). The development of critical thinking: Does college make a difference? *Journal of College Student Development, 30*, 19-26.

Paul, R. (1995). *Critical thinking: How to prepare students for a rapidly changing world.* In J. Willsen & A.J.A. Binker (Eds.). Santa Rosa, CA: The Foundation for Critical Thinking.

Paul, R. (1992). *Critical thinking: What every person needs to survive in a rapidly changing world* (2nd ed.). (A.J.A. Binker, Ed.). Santa Rosa, CA: The Foundation for Critical Thinking.

Paul, R. W., Elder, L., & Bartell, T. (1997). *California teacher preparation for instruction in critical thinking: Research findings and policy recommendations.* Sacramento, CA: California Commission on Teacher Credentialing.

Potts, B., (1994). Strategies for teaching critical thinking [microform]. Washington, DC: Dept. of Education Catholic University of America ERIC Clearinghouse on Assessment and Evaluation.

Ramsden, P., (1992). *Learning to teach in higher education.* London; New York: Routledge.

Ramsden, P. (2003). *Learning to teach in higher education* (2nd Edition). London; New York: Routledge.

Raths, L. E. (1986). *Teaching for thinking: Theory, strategies, and activities for the classroom* (2nd ed.). New York: Teachers College Columbia University.

Saroyan, A., & Amundsen, C. (2004). *Rethinking teaching in higher education: From a course design workshop to a faculty development framework.* Sterling, Va.: Stylus Publishing.

Scriven, M., & Paul, R. (2001). *Defining critical thinking,* Retrieved October 5, 2003 from http://www.criticalthinking.org/aboutCT/definingCT.shtml

Sloffer, S. J., Dueber, B., & Duffy, T. M. (1999). *Using asynchronous conferencing to promote critical thinking: two implementations in higher education.* In the Proceedings of the 32nd Hawaii International Conference on System Sciences. Maui, Hawaii.

Spaulding, S. C., & Kleiner, K. (1992). The relationship of college and critical thinking: Are critical thinkers attracted or created by college disciplines? *College Student Journal, 26,* 162-166.

Stevens, D. D., & Levi, A.J. (2005). *Introduction to rubrics: An assessment tool to save grading time, convey effective feedback and promote student learning.* Sterling, VA: Stylus Publishing.

Thibault, C. & Van Gyn, G. (2003). *Teaching for critical thinking: Examples from colleagues at the University of Victoria.* Unpublished manuscript. University of Victoria, British Columbia, Canada.

Tsui, L. (2002). Fostering critical thinking through effective pedagogy: Evidence from four institutional case studies. *The Journal of Higher Education, 73*(6), 740-763.

Vermunt, J. D. (2003). The power of learning environments and the quality of student learning. In S. Strauss, E. De Corte, R. Wegerif & K. Littleton (Series Eds.) and E. De Corte, L. Vershalffel, N. Entwistle & J. van Merrienboer (Vol. Eds.), *Advances in learning and instruction: Vol. 13. Powerful learning environments: Unravelling basic components and dimensions* (pp. 109-124). Amsterdam: Pergamon.

Vygotsky, L. S. (1978). *Mind and society: The development of higher mental processes.* Cambridge, MA: Harvard University Press.

About STLHE

A message from Julia Christensen Hughes, President

The Society for Teaching and Learning in Higher Education (STLHE) is a national association of academics interested in the improvement of teaching and learning in higher education. STLHE has four primary strategic directions:

- Advancing the scholarship of teaching
- Advocating for excellence in teaching and learning
- Achieving inclusivity in all our activities
- Alliances – supporting the formation of strategic partnerships

In pursuit of these four strategic directions, the Society presents an annual conference co-hosted by a different Canadian university each year. The conference is renowned for its practical and interactive approach; attendees include university and college administrators, faculty, educational developers, and graduate students. STLHE also coordinates the country's most prestigious national teaching awards programs: the 3M Teaching Fellowships, cosponsored by 3M Canada, in recognition of teaching excellence and educational leadership and the Alan Blizzard Award, co-sponsored by McGraw Hill Ryerson, Canada in recognition of excellence in collaborative projects that improve student learning. In addition, the Society produces the Green Guide Series – publications which address the most common challenges faculty encounter in their teaching practice.

To keep its members informed, STLHE produces a bi-annual newsletter, Teaching and Learning in Higher Education and hosts an extremely active listserv—the Forum for Teaching and Learning in Higher Education. Listserv members are faculty and educational developers from post-secondary institutions across Canada and beyond.

STLHE is organized by a Steering Committee, an enthusiastic group of faculty and educational developers who have either been elected by their peers or appointed in recognition of the essential role they play in supporting the Society's work.

Elected positions include a president, past president and regional representatives from: Newfoundland-New Brunswick-Prince Edward Island; Nova Scotia; Francophone Quebec; Anglophone Quebec; Ontario South-West; Ontario North-East; Ontario Central; Manitoba-Saskatchewan; Alberta; and British Columbia.

In addition to these elected positions, the Chairs of the 3M Teaching Fellows Council and Educational Developers Caucus—two very important groups that are officially constituted within STLHE—serve on the Steering Committee, along with the Program Coordinator for the 3M Teaching Fellows Program, Chair of our Publications Committee, and Treasurer.

STLHE Membership

If you are interested in a forum for the exchange of ideas and information on post-secondary teaching and learning; if you believe that teaching is important and that dedication to its improvement should be recognized; if you feel that the road to professional improvement is best walked in the company of enthusiastic peers; then you should join the Society.

Membership is open to anyone who supports the aims of the Society. Information on individual and institutional memberships can be obtained from the Society.

Julia Christensen Hughes (jchriste@uoguelph.ca)
c/o Teaching Support Services
University of Guelph
Guelph, Ontario   N1G 2W1
www.stlhe.ca

Ordering Green Guides
To order please contact

The Book Store at Western
University Community Centre
The University of Western Ontario
London, Ontario   N6A 3K7
Phone: (519) 661-3520
Fax: (519) 661-3673
E-mail: bkstor@uwo.ca
Web: www.bookstore.uwo.ca